Sunset
Woodworking Projects II

By the Editors of Sunset Books and Sunset Magazine

Lane Publishing Co. · Menlo Park, California

Something for everyone

You may have taken up woodworking purely for the pleasure of crafting— or because you appreciate custom-made furniture and accessories. Either way, you'll find in this book a woodworker's treasury of good ideas.

In 1975, Sunset published the second edition of *Woodworking Projects I*, which continues to be one of our most popular titles. But many of its readers have wished for even more great projects from Sunset—and here they are. Volume II includes simple to challenging pieces for every skill level, beginner to advanced. Each unique, handsome design comes with clear directions, and the final chapter gives background information on tools, terms, and techniques.

We gratefully acknowledge the many woodworkers who contributed their time and talents to this volume— especially Rob Ellis, Bob Nyden, David A. Pedersen, and Peter Santulli. We extend special thanks to Rebecca La Brum, who carefully copy edited the manuscript, and to Scott Atkinson, who checked it for technical accuracy. Finally, we'd like to thank Abacus and Roger Reynolds Nursery for their generosity in providing props for use in our photographs.

Coordinating Editor
Alice Rich Hallowell

Technical Editor
Donald Rutherford

Contributing Editor
Don Vandervort

Design
Roger Flanagan

Illustrations
Bill Oetinger
Mark Pechenik

Photography
Stephen Marley

Photo Stylist
JoAnn Masaoka

Cover: Ways to put your craft to good use: Delight youngsters with colorful building blocks (page 47) or a super scooter plane (page 54). Enhance your living room with a handsome coffee table (page 33), or fill a practical need in your kitchen with a sleek knife rack (page 8). Photograph by Stephen Marley. Cover design by Naganuma Design & Direction.

Editor, Sunset Books: Elizabeth L. Hogan

Fifth printing April 1990

Copyright © 1984, Lane Publishing Co., Menlo Park, CA 94025. First edition. World rights reserved. No part of this publication may be reproduced by any mechanical, photographic, or electronic process, or in the form of a phonographic recording, nor may it be stored in a retrieval system, transmitted, or otherwise copied for public or private use without prior written permission from the publisher. Library of Congress Catalog Card Number: 83-82502. ISBN 0-376-04888-3. Lithographed in the United States.

CONTENTS

HOUSEHOLD ACCESSORIES
4

An assortment of easy projects for the weekend woodworker

HOBBY & CRAFT PROJECTS
58

Something special for an artist, gymnast, sewer, or collector

FURNITURE
20

Tables galore, plus great beds & chairs— even a computer center

YARD & GARDEN ACCESSORIES
70

Birdhouse, mailbox, lanterns, whirligig & other outdoor delights

CHILDREN'S FURNITURE & TOYS
40

Small-fry necessities: boats, blocks, swings, tables, a sandbox & more

TOOLS & TECHNIQUES
81

From wood selection to sanding & finishing— the basics of the craft

INDEX
96

HOUSEHOLD ACCESSORIES

NAPKIN RINGS

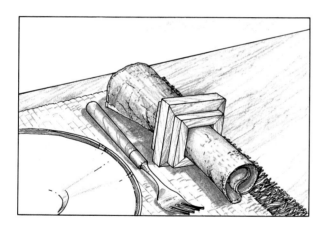

These elegant-looking wooden napkin rings are surprisingly easy to make: all you do is cut and glue pine molding together. We used some of the simplest and least expensive moldings available to make the rings illustrated here. For more variations, look through the molding racks at your lumber supplier.

The rings made of cove and stop moldings have butt joints; glue long lengths of molding together to form hollow tubes. After the glue is dry, cut the tubes into sections about 1¼ inches long. Use a radial-arm or table saw with a planer blade for a smooth finish on the cut faces.

The corner guard and shoe moldings have mitered corners, so you must cut and miter individual pieces and glue them together (see page 88 for information on miter joints). Make the inside edges about 1¼ inches long.

Sand the completed rings; then finish with a polyurethane penetrating oil sealer.

Design: Rick Morrall.

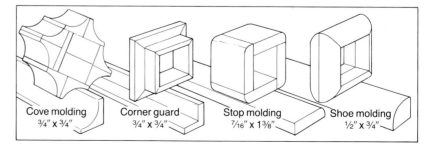

Cove molding ¾" x ¾"   Corner guard ¾" x ¾"   Stop molding 7/16" x 1⅜"   Shoe molding ½" x ¾"

SERVING BOARD 6-PACK

Rack up your serving boards on their own compact stand so they're always handy when you need them. There's a size for every function in this set of six boards in three graduated sizes.

Materials list

For 6 serving boards and 1 stand:
8′ of 1 by 6 clear pine or other clear species
8″ of 1″ hardwood dowel
6″ of 2 by 6 clear pine or fir
Glue

Begin by marking and cutting the 1 by 6 into pieces of the following lengths:

2 @ 8½″
2 @ 10½″
2 @ 12½″
1 @ 14″

On each board, carefully mark a point 1½ inches from one end and exactly centered. Mark another centered point 2¾ inches from the same end. Place the sharp end of a compass on this second point and draw a semicircle across the top of each board. Cut along each curved line.

Using the 1½-inch mark as the center point, drill a 1-inch hole in the 14-inch board. Then drill a 1⅛-inch hole through each of the six remaining boards, using the 1½-inch mark as the center point. You must locate each hole precisely and make the cuts perpendicular for the boards to hang properly.

Sandwich all the boards together with the sides aligned, placing the 14-inch board in the middle and graduating the others down to the 8½-inch boards on the outsides. Slip the dowel through the holes in the boards to keep all pieces aligned. Clamp the boards together, using wood scraps on the outsides to prevent clamp marks.

Sand the sides and top curves of this block of boards until they all match. Remove the clamps and do any final sanding. Set the serving boards aside.

Cut a ¾-inch-wide, ¾-inch-deep dado across the center of the 2 by 6 base. Use a dado attachment on a table saw, or make several passes with a regular blade set at a height of 1 inch.

Sand this base piece and both ends of the dowel, rounding the dowel ends. Glue the 14-inch board into the base notch; glue the dowel into the hole in this upright so both ends extend equally. When the glue is dry, finish the serving boards and stand as desired.

Design: Diana Bunce.

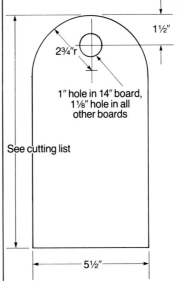

1½″

2¾″r

1″ hole in 14″ board,
1⅛″ hole in all
other boards

See cutting list

5½″

MESSAGE CENTER

Use this wall-mounted message center to keep phone books and writing supplies within easy reach of your telephone. It's a handy storage spot for household keys, too. A bulletin board and an erasable marking board on the front provide ample space for easy-to-find messages.

Materials list

12' of 1 by 4 clear pine or fir
1' of ³⁄₁₆" hardwood dowel
30" by 48" piece of ¾" birch plywood
12¹³⁄₁₆" by 21¼" piece of ¼" sheet cork
1 erasable marker sheet, 12¹³⁄₁₆" by 21¼"
24" of ¾" piano hinge
2 6" stay supports
2 magnetic catches
2 wall-mounting brackets with ¾" and 2" screws
4d (1½") finishing nails
24 flathead woodscrews, 1¾" by #8
Glue
Contact cement

Cut the plywood for the back, door, and top front pieces. Round the outer corners of the top front and the door to a ¾-inch radius (see drawing below).

On the front face of the back piece, lightly mark the locations of the 1 by 4 framing pieces. Cut eight 1¼-inch-long dowels and glue them to the back in ³⁄₁₆-inch-wide, ⅜-inch-deep holes set 1 inch apart.

Cut the 1 by 4 into framing pieces as shown. Cut a ¾-inch-deep, 3½-inch-long dado in one end of a divider. Drill and countersink pilot holes for 1¾-inch wood-screws in the back; then glue and screw the framing pieces in place. Also glue and nail the joints between the 1 by 4s. Cut and glue two plywood pieces and a 1 by 4 shelf to fit between the dividers.

Glue and screw the top front in place, making sure the screws will be hidden by the bulletin board cork. Cut a 21¼-inch piece of hinge and screw it to the bottom 1 by 4. Center the door piece over the hinge and screw in place. Mount the stay supports to the sides of the frame and the door, making sure that the door (in the open position) is at a 90° angle to the cabinet and that the supports don't hit the back when the door is closed. Install magnetic catches to hold the door shut.

Apply the finish of your choice and let it dry. Then, using contact cement, glue the cork to the top front and the marker sheet to the door front (follow the manufacturer's instructions). Mask any plywood areas that shouldn't be covered with the contact cement.

Design: Don Vandervort.

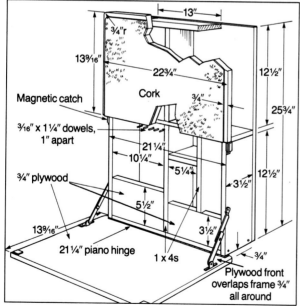

Magnetic catch

Cork

13"

¾"r

13⁹⁄₁₆"

22¾"

12½"

25¾"

¾"

³⁄₁₆" x 1¼" dowels, 1" apart

21¼"

10¼"

5¼"

3½"

12½"

¾" plywood

5½"

13⁹⁄₁₆"

21¼" piano hinge

3½"

3½"

¾"

1 x 4s

Plywood front overlaps frame ¾" all around

SPICE RACK

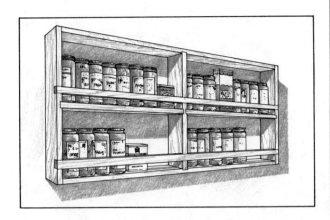

Is your spice collection bursting out of its present space? This easy-to-make rack offers the abundant shelving space that no serious spice collector should be without. You can easily adapt its dimensions to fit your available space and the size of your spice jars.

The drawing below gives the dimensions for a rack that holds jars measuring 1⅞ by 4⅜ inches; each double-shelf section holds 18 of these jars between the uprights. Add as many sections as you need.

Make the uprights and the shelves from any species of 1 by 3. Use standard ½ by ¾-inch molding for the retaining strips, or rip strips from 1-inch-thick lumber.

Cut ¾-inch-wide, ½-inch-deep dadoes on the fronts of the uprights; also cut ¾-inch-wide, ¼-inch-deep dadoes on the sides of the uprights for the shelves and on the top and bottom shelves for the uprights (see "Dado joints," page 88). Glue the pieces together and clamp them until dry.

Sand all the surfaces and apply the finish of your choice. Mount the shelves on the wall with 2½ by 2½-inch angle brackets attached to the bottom and middle shelves. If you attach the brackets with the vertical legs up, the jars will conceal them.

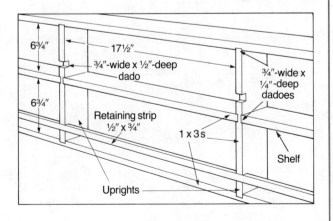

COOLING RACK

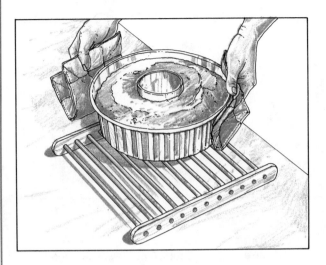

There's no need to banish this cooling rack to the back of the cupboard when its job is done; it's handsome enough to hang on the wall for display.

To make a 12-inch-square rack, you'll need two pieces of pine or redwood lattice (each about ¼ by 1½ by 12 inches), 12 feet of 5/16-inch hardwood dowel, glue, and polyurethane penetrating oil sealer.

Cut the dowel into 1-foot lengths. Mark the center of each lattice piece, then mark five points an inch apart in each direction for the 11 holes. Drill a 5/16-inch hole through each mark. Sand both lattice pieces. Put glue inside the holes on one piece and push the dowels into place. Apply glue inside the holes on the other side piece and carefully fit the dowels into the holes (it's easier with an extra pair of hands to help). Gently tap the side piece down onto the dowels; wipe off excess glue.

Place the rack flat on a level surface; put a board and a weight on top of it. (This prevents the rack from twisting, which can cause it to tip.) When the glue is dry, finish the rack with a coat of oil sealer.

Design: William Crosby.

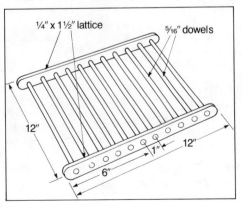

BLADE RACK

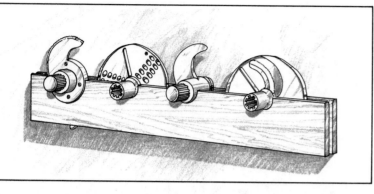

Keep your food processor blades safely and neatly stored in an easy-access rack. (You may need to modify the dimensions to fit the blades of your particular processor.)

For the rack front and back, you'll need two 22-inch lengths of reversible baseboard molding, such as ash. To make the four custom-sized cutouts, lay your food processor blades on one of the molding strips so the blade hubs are bisected by the top edge of the molding. Space the blades so they won't knock against each other; then mark semicircles around the hubs. Cut out the semicircles and sand them smooth.

Cut a pair of small, narrow spacers (¼ to ½ inch thick, depending on the thickness of your slicing and shredding disks) to fit between the front and back moldings at the ends of the rack. Also cut a couple of wider spacers, ¼ to ½ inch thick; glued to the back molding, they'll help keep the thinner chopping and mixing blades in position.

Assemble the pieces with glue, then clamp or weight until dry. Finish the wood with a polyurethane penetrating oil sealer, stain, or paint. You can screw the rack to the wall or fit it with a pair of metal saw-toothed picture hangers.

Design: Rick Morrall.

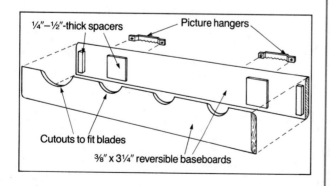

¼"–½"-thick spacers
Picture hangers
Cutouts to fit blades
⅜" x 3¼" reversible baseboards

KNIFE RACK

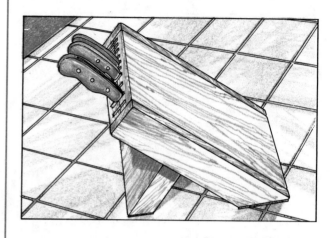

Custom-build this sturdy rack to fit your supply of kitchen knives. You'll need 30 inches of 2 by 8 hardwood, 26 inches of 1 by 4 hardwood, and a piece of ⅛-inch cork.

From the 2 by 8, cut a 23-inch piece (for body of rack). Cut the foot from the remaining 2 by 8, mitering one end so the short face is 4½ inches long, as shown. Round all edges of the foot.

Cut a series of lengthwise grooves in one wide face of the 23-inch 2 by 8. (Cut grooves slightly more than half as deep as your knife blades are wide.) Round long edges of face opposite grooved face. Mark across center of grooved face; cut piece in two at a 45° angle.

Glue and screw straight end of foot to face side of smaller grooved piece. Then glue grooved pieces together, aligning grooves and edges. After glue is dry, round remaining square edges. Cut two 13-inch side pieces from the 1 by 4; miter one end of each, round all edges, and glue to grooved section.

Sand surfaces smooth and apply finish as desired. Cut cork to fit bottoms of rack and foot; glue in place.

Design: Donald Rutherford.

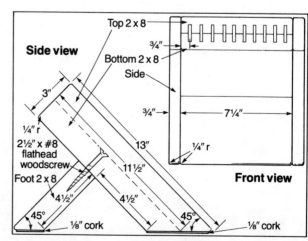

Side view

Top 2 x 8
¾"
Bottom 2 x 8
Side
3"
¼" r
2½" x #8 flathead woodscrew
Foot 2 x 8
13"
11½"
4½"
4½"
45°
45°
¼" r
7¼"
⅛" cork
⅛" cork
Front view

HANGING POT RACK

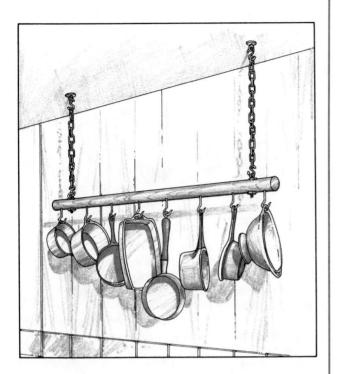

Keep your cookware within easy reach and add a decorative touch to your kitchen with this simple, lightweight pot rack.

To support the weight of the pots, secure the rack to ceiling joists, not to gypsum board. Locate the joists (they're probably 16 inches apart) and twist 4-inch eyescrews into them through the ceiling; space the screws 32 inches apart for a 44-inch rack. (If the joists run at right angles to the rack, you may be limited to 16, 24, 32, or 48-inch spacing.)

In a 1½-inch round, drill holes the same distance apart as the eyescrews. Assemble eyebolts in the holes with washers and nuts. Screw eyehooks for hanging pots into the lower side of the round; then suspend it with S-hooks and metal chains. Adjust to a convenient height.

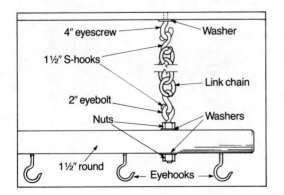

OVEN RACK PUSH-PULL

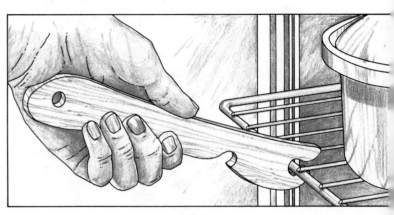

We first saw a device like this in a collection of Shaker furniture. Hang it near your oven; then use it to slide hot oven racks in and out without burning your fingers.

Cut both the curved "Shaker" pattern and the simpler rectangular shape from strips of ⅜-inch-thick oak.

To make the curved push-pull, first trace the pattern onto the wood (see drawing below). Next, drill three ⅜-inch holes in the wood—one at the base of the handle (for hanging), one at the side (for the pulling notch), and one at the end (for the pushing notch). Then cut out the shape with a coping or saber saw; the half-circles that remain form the ends of the two notches.

Cut the rectangular push-pull with a coping or fine-toothed crosscut handsaw. Then drill a hanging hole at one end.

After cutting push-pulls, sand all surfaces and finish with several coats of a polyurethane penetrating oil sealer. If you like, thread a piece of leather thong through the hanging hole and knot it into a loop.

Design: William Crosby.

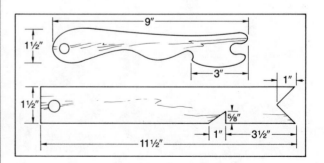

TILE TRIVET

Protect your table from the heat of serving dishes with a good-looking tile trivet.

You'll need one 8-inch tile and 40 inches of 1 by 2 clear hardwood such as oak, maple, or cherry. Use scraps of the same or a contrasting wood to make splines.

First, cut a rabbet in the 1 by 2 (see drawing below). Then cut the 1 by 2 into four equal pieces to frame the tile, mitering both ends of each piece.

Cut ⅛-inch-wide, ¼-inch-deep grooves for the splines on the mitered faces. Cut a ⅛ by ½-inch spline for each corner.

Check the fit by assembling the pieces without glue. Then glue the pieces and clamp until dry. Then trim and sand the splines flush with the frame and round the outer edges of the frame. Sand the frame smooth; apply the finish of your choice. Glue the tile to the frame. Finally, glue small felt pads to the bottom corners of the trivet to protect your table from scratches.

Design: Donald Rutherford.

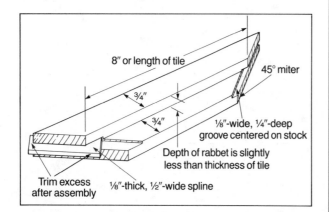

8″ or length of tile

45° miter

¾″

¾″

⅛″-wide, ¼″-deep groove centered on stock

Depth of rabbet is slightly less than thickness of tile

Trim excess after assembly

⅛″-thick, ½″-wide spline

TOTE BOXES

For carrying odds and ends, there's nothing handier than the traditional carpenter's toolbox. You can easily adapt the design to make lightweight tote boxes that are useful around the house and garden.

The garden tote box has two-inch-high sides, low enough to allow easy access to garden supplies. You can also use it to carry tools and supplies for a backyard barbecue.

The narrow under-the-sink tote box takes less storage space than the garden tote box. Its high sides securely hold household tools and cleaning equipment.

For each of the tote boxes shown here, you'll need five pieces of ½-inch plywood, plus ¾-inch hardwood dowel for the handle. Either glue the dowels into drilled holes or fasten them to the ends with glue and long woodscrews. You can follow the dimensions in the drawing below, or adapt the box size to your own needs.

A few minutes of sanding prepares the surface for finishing and reduces the chance of splinters. Seal the tote boxes with a clear finish or paint them as colorfully as you like.

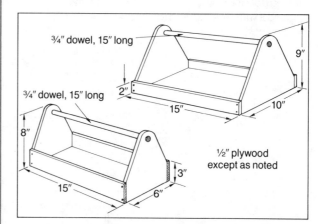

¾″ dowel, 15″ long

9″

2″

¾″ dowel, 15″ long

15″

10″

8″

15″

3″

6″

½″ plywood except as noted

STEPSTOOL CARRYALL

If you store often-used housecleaning materials all in one place, you'll be able to complete many small jobs in a hurry. And when that one place is portable, household tasks become easier still.

This stepstool carryall is a place to store and a way to carry, all in one. It's roomy enough to hold most of the supplies you need, from cleansers and sponges to a roll of paper towels.

Cart the carryall from job to job and use it as a stepstool when you need a boost to clean light fixtures, windows, and other out-of-reach areas.

You can easily make this household helper from a 2 by 4-foot piece of ¾-inch plywood (see drawing below). Join all pieces with glue and 6d (2-inch) finishing nails. The two 8 by 16-inch steps are a comfortable width to stand on; and since there's no overhang, there's little chance of the stepstool tipping.

Attach 4-inch-high panels at the front and back to keep the contents securely inside. Glue and nail a plywood scrap under the front of the top step to provide a handhold at the center balance point (or cut a handhold in the top step).

Cover the steps with anti-slip strips. Screw rubber feet into the base at each corner to protect your floor from scratches.

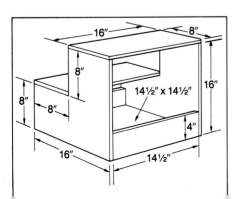

MIRROR & MAILBOX

Add beauty and practicality to your entryway wall with this mirror that doubles as a mail pickup.

Start by ripping the rounded edges off a 6-foot 1 by 8 to make the board 7 inches wide. Cut five pieces, mitering the corner joints at front and top. Along the top, side, and bottom pieces, ½ inch from the back edge, cut a groove ⁵⁄₁₆ inch deep and ³⁄₁₆ inch wide. Sand all surfaces, then glue and nail together the front, side and bottom pieces. Slide the 17 by 26-inch mirror into the groove; then glue and nail on the top.

Install eyescrews and picture wire on the back and hang on two picture hooks about 9 inches apart.

Design: Peter O. Whiteley.

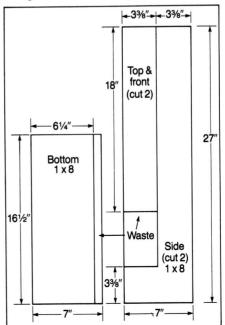

BATHROOM FITTINGS

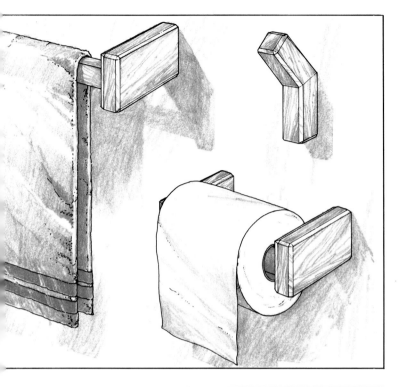

These simple, good-looking fittings are designed for use on a wood-paneled wall. The towel rack, hook, and paper holder are all cut from ¾-inch oak board and attached to the paneling with glue and dowels. Assemble each fitting as directed; then attach it to the wall, following the instructions for wall mounting.

TOWEL RACK. For the brackets, cut two 2½ by 4-inch pieces of oak (see Drawing 1). Bevel all the edges except those on the surfaces that attach to the wall. For the rod, cut a ¾-inch-wide strip of oak to the length you need and bevel the edges.

To chisel sockets for the rod, first mark the brackets: place the end of the rod on each bracket and trace its outline with a pencil. Chisel out sockets about ⅜ inch deep. Attach one bracket to the wall and hold the towel rack in place in its socket; then position and attach the other bracket.

PAPER HOLDER. Cut two 2½ by 4-inch brackets (see Drawing 1). Bevel all edges except those that will lie against the wall. Drill slightly oversize holes centered 1 inch from the front inside edge of both brackets to hold a spring-loaded insert (sold at hardware stores).

HOOK. The protruding part extends out from the wall at a 45° angle and measures 1¼ inches along its upper surface (see Drawing 2). The surface that attaches to the wall is 2 inches long. Saw out the entire piece, then bevel all the edges except those on the surface that lies against the wall.

WALL MOUNTING. To attach the fittings, drill holes in the wall paneling and the fittings, making them large enough to accept short lengths of ¼-inch dowel (two pieces of dowel for each hook or bracket). Glue and position as in Drawings 1 and 2. Finish the fittings with a clear polyurethane sealer before installing, using several coats on the towel rod and hook to protect them from moisture.

Design: Gordon Hammond.

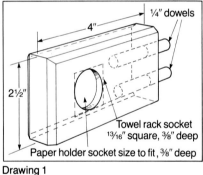

¼" dowels

4"

2½"

Towel rack socket
¹³⁄₁₆" square, ⅜" deep

Paper holder socket size to fit, ⅜" deep

Drawing 1

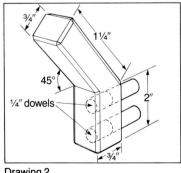

¾"

1¼"

45°

¼" dowels

2"

¾"

Drawing 2

READING LAMP

Unsightly, dangling lamp cords aren't a problem with this handsome floor lamp: the lamp post, made of quarter-rounds, conceals the cord in its hollow center. You put weights in the base to make this a sturdy piece of furniture.

Materials list

16′ of 1″ quarter-round pine molding: 4 @ 4′
3′ of 1 by 12 clear pine
Glue
Weights (BB's, fishing weights, or lead shot)
8 flathead woodscrews, 2″ by #8
Masking tape
Cord and plug
½″ by 5″ nipple
3-way socket
Decorative washer and nut
12″ harp
Lamp shade
Polyurethane penetrating oil sealer

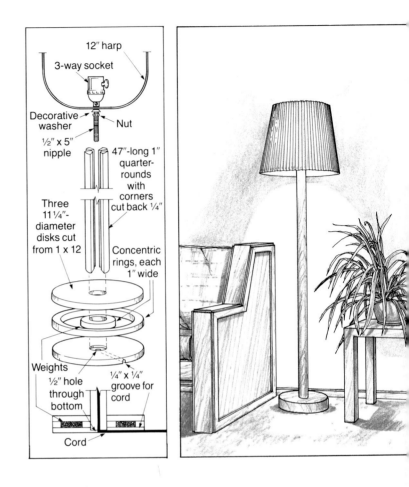

The base begins as three 11¼-inch disks cut from the pine 1 by 12 (see drawing). With a circle cutter, cut a 2-inch hole through the center of two of the disks. Also cut a 2-inch hole halfway through the third (or bottom) disk; then chisel out the hole to the depth of this cut. For the lamp cord, cut a ¼ by ¼-inch groove from the edge of the bottom disk to the center and a ½-inch hole through the bottom center.

Cut the center disk into two concentric rings—an inner and an outer one, each 1 inch wide—to provide space for the weights that stabilize the lamp. Glue these rings to the bottom disk, the inner ring flush with the 2-inch center hole and the outer ring flush with the outer edge. Fill in the space with weights; then glue on the top disk. When glue is dry, secure assembly from the bottom with four 2-inch woodscrews and sand all surfaces smooth.

Make the lamp post from four 4-foot-long pieces of quarter-round molding. On a table saw with the blade set at 45°, rip ¼ inch off the corner of each piece to create the space for the cord. Glue the four pieces together and wrap the post with masking tape; leave tape on until the glue is dry.

To complete the lamp, remove tape and sand the post smooth. Spread some glue in the base; then insert the post. Secure it from below and bring it to true verti-

cal with four 2-inch woodscrews. Next, thread the cord through the bottom hole and up the post; staple the cord in the groove.

Assemble the socket, harp, decorative washer, and nut on the nipple; then feed the cord through the nipple and connect it to the socket. Push the nipple into the post top and attach the plug to the cord. Finish the lamp post and base with three coats of a polyurethane penetrating oil sealer.

Design: William Crosby.

GEOMETRIC WINE RACK

A triangular shelving system inside a rectangular frame makes a good-looking wine rack for a dozen bottles of wine.

You'll need about 8 feet of 1 by 12 pine (or any clear wood) and 20 4d (1½-inch) finishing nails. Cut the wood according to the dimensions in the drawing below, cutting both ends of each of the dividers at a 45° angle. Sand all surfaces. Assemble the rack with finishing nails and glue. After the glue is dry, apply the finish of your choice.

Design: Rick Morrall.

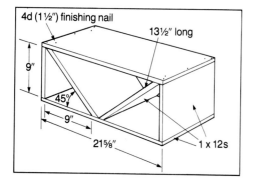

STACKING WINE RACK

Easy to stack in multiple layers and easy to store in a small space when not in use, this wine rack is an ideal gift for any wine lover. Three layers of racks hold a case of wine; you can add or subtract layers depending on your current inventory. You'll need 1 by 4s for this project; use clear wood such as redwood, pine, or fir, or hardwood such as mahogany or oak.

The semicircular cut-out areas in this rack system cradle wine bottles in proper storage position. Cut the half-circles in the 1 by 4s as shown below.

Cut ¾-inch-wide, ⅜-inch-deep dadoes, 1 inch in from the ends, on the lower edges of the two top-level boards, on the upper and lower edges of the middle boards, and on the upper edges of the bottom boards (see "Dado joints," page 88). Also dado both edges of the 10-inch-long connectors, 1 inch in from the ends. Cut all dadoes tight; sand the board faces, if necessary, until boards fit snugly. Sand all other surfaces and finish as desired.

Design: Rick Morrall.

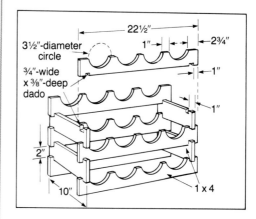

BUILT-IN WINE RACK

Strong and stable, this wine rack system can support the weight of a large collection of wine. Make the rack to fit your needs and available space, using our measurements as a guide; our rack system fits a space 87 inches high and 62½ inches wide.

From 3 by 3 milled lumber, cut four corner posts, each 87 inches long. On two sides of each post, cut ¾-inch grooves as shown in Drawing 1.

Cut 12 front and 12 rear bottle support racks 59 inches long from 1-inch milled lumber (see Drawing 2). To make two racks at a time, center and drill or cut the holes on a board that is double the width of each rack; then rip the boards in half.

Spacing the racks are ¾ by ¾-inch wood spacers fitted into the corner post grooves (see Drawing 3). The front spacers are 4½ inches long, the rear ones 3½ inches, to keep bottoms of front and rear racks level. When you cut the spacers, use a jig to ensure exact lengths.

Use 1 by 6s for the side panels, and 1 by 2s and a 1 by 8 (notched for the corner posts) for the top. Screw vertical 2 by 2s at the center of the front and rear racks for midpoint support. Anchor the rack to the wall with lag screws.

Design: Tom Wilson.

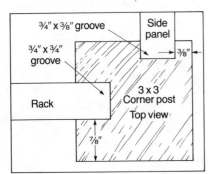

Drawing 1

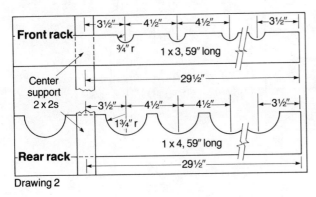

Drawing 2

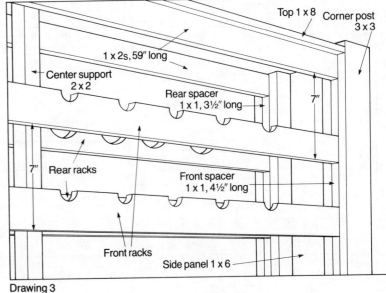

Drawing 3

STEPSTOOL CHAIR

Inspired by a Victorian stepstool, this efficient piece of equipment has a piano hinge mounted between the first and second seat slats. The hinge allows the chair to swing over and convert into a three-step stepstool. The seat is 16 inches high; the stepstool's top step is 24 inches high.

Materials list

18' of 1 by 4 fir: 3 @ 4', 1 @ 6'
10' of 1 by 3 fir
2' of 1 by 2 fir
4' of 1 by 6 fir
16"-long piano hinge, with screws
52 flathead woodscrews, 1¼" by #8
Glue

Cut lumber according to the measurements in Drawing 1. For all joints, drill and countersink pilot holes; then glue and screw pieces together (see Drawing 2).

To construct the front leg assembly, attach the diagonal supports A to the front legs B; screw from the insides of the legs. Stand the legs on the floor or other smooth surface. Using a carpenter's square, measure up 7¼ inches and draw a horizontal line on the inside of each diagonal support. Align the edge of a step support C with this line, then screw through the step supports into the diagonals. Next, attach a step D and the front

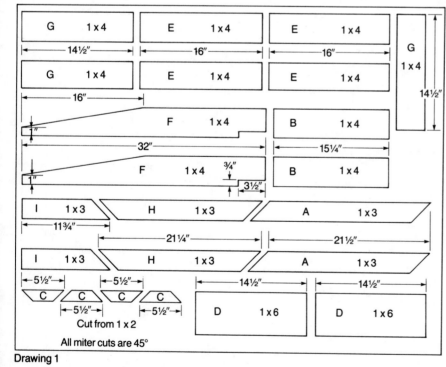

Drawing 1

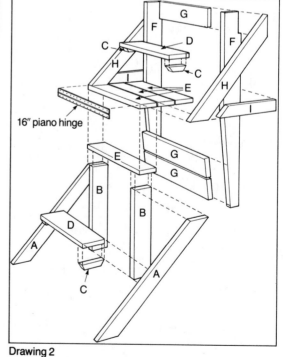

16" piano hinge

Drawing 2

seat slat E; their top edges will be 8 and 16 inches from the ground, respectively.

To construct the back assembly, first attach the two back slats G to the tapered part of the back legs F. The slats are positioned ⅜ inch from the tips of the tapers and have a ⅜-inch gap between them. Next, fit the brace G into the notches on F.

Position this back assembly with the front leg assembly as it will be when finished and in the chair position (see drawing of finished project at far left). The bottom tip of each diagonal support A should be flush with the edge of the brace G.

Rest each rear diagonal support H on a front diagonal support A; the bottom of H should be flush with the lower back edge of the back assembly, and the top end should align with the end of the front diagonal support A. Clamp each diagonal H to the back assembly in this position and screw together, screwing from the insides of the back legs F into the diagonals.

Now attach the seat supports I; the top edges should be 15¼ inches up from the ground. The diagonal edges of these pieces should butt cleanly against the short edges of the rear diagonals H. Glue the butted edges of each piece; then screw from the insides of the back legs into the other ends.

Separate the two assemblies. Set a seat slat E on top of the slat already in place on the front leg assembly. Join the two slats at their edges with the piano hinge, barrel facing out (you'll probably have to cut a standard 24-inch hinge down to 16 inches with a hacksaw). Set the back assembly in place again on the front leg assembly, swing the hinged slat over onto the tops of the rear diagonal supports H, and screw it into place. Attach the other two slats E behind this one, spacing them ⅜ inch apart.

Finally, attach a step D for the top step. First, swing the seat over into the stepstool position. Measure up 23¼ inches from the ground and draw a horizontal line on the inside of each rear diagonal support H. Then attach the step supports C, screwing through them into the diagonals. Attach the step D to the supports.

When you pick up the chair, friction should hold it together, but if it tends to swing open, you can attach a hook and eye on the inside between the diagonals A and H to hold it in the chair position.

Design: William Crosby.

BOOK RACK

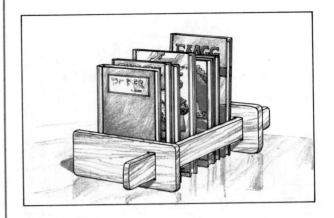

This freestanding book rack is especially suited for holding the large books that can often overpower small bookends. The ends of the rack slide apart along the spine to hold more books, but hold firm when books lean against them.

To make the book rack, the only thing you need is a 24-inch-long piece of 1 by 8; any kind of wood will do. For a longer rack, use 1 by 3 stock for the spine and 1 by 6 for the ends.

Cut the pieces as shown below. Cut the hole to the exact dimensions of the end of the spine. To do this, position the spine on each end piece, centering it about 2 inches in from narrow end; then carefully trace the outline. Cut just inside the lines with a coping or saber saw, then file the sides smooth to size with a wood rasp. The spine should just barely slide through the holes, so a minimum of racking force will hold the ends firmly in place (sand the sides of the holes as necessary).

Finally, sand all surfaces of the rack and finish with several coats of a polyurethane penetrating oil sealer.

Design: Gary Williams.

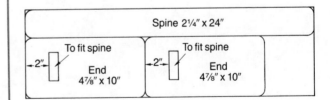

SLIDE-ON BOOKEND

Propping up an ever-toppling row of books can be a constant battle. The usual remedy is a metal bookend or a pile of heavy books—but here's a more efficient alternative. This one-piece wooden bookend slides easily onto a bookshelf and stays put.

The dimensions given in the drawing below will make a bookend that fits on a ¾-inch shelf; you can change the slot size and the overall dimensions to suit your needs.

Cut the bookend from 2 by 10 oak with the grain running parallel to the shelf for extra strength. Don't use softer woods such as pine, fir, or redwood—bookends made from these tend to break at the closed end of the slot.

Cut the slot ¹⁄₁₆ inch wider than the shelf's thickness. As the books lean outward against the bookend, it will tilt slightly and bind into place.

Design: Tom Keller.

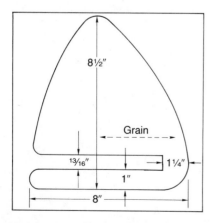

BOOK & RECORD RACKS

BOOK RACK. Dowels form adjustable tracks for this book rack. Use it to hold a few favorite cook books or desk-top reference books. We provide a specific dowel length, but you can adjust the length to fit your needs.

Materials list

2 8″ squares of ³⁄₁₆″ clear acrylic
2′ of 1 by 3 maple
2′ of 1″ hardwood dowel
4 roundhead woodscrews, ½″ by #3

Note: If you plan to cut the acrylic yourself, use a fine plywood blade on your power saw. For the 1-inch holes, use a Forstner or multi-spur bit (see page 87).

Cut two 8-inch end pieces from the maple 1 by 3; cut the dowel into two 12-inch lengths.

Leave the protective paper on the acrylic sheets until you've completed all the cuts and bores. To ensure that the holes are aligned, clamp all the acrylic and maple end pieces together with a scrap piece of wood on the bottom. Drill a 1-inch hole ¾ inch up and 1½ inches in from each end of the end pieces. Drilling is a critical part of this project; if the holes aren't cut perpendicular or don't line up, the supports won't slide smoothly along

RECORD RACK. The end plates of this record rack are immobile, providing critical support for the records. The middle panel slides along the rack to hold records upright and prevent warping.

Materials list

4′ of 1 by 12 hardwood
8′ of 1″ hardwood dowel: 4 @ 2′
1′ of ⅜″ hardwood dowel
Glue

Cut the hardwood into three 12-inch-long pieces for the end plates and the sliding panel. Mark 1-inch dowel hole locations on one plate as shown in the drawing at right. Clamp the three pieces together and drill the four 1-inch diameter holes through all thicknesses. Drilling is a critical part of this project; if the holes aren't cut perpendicular or don't line up, the supports won't slide smoothly along the dowels.

Finish the wood, if desired; then slide the pieces onto the 1-inch dowels. Glue and dowel the two end plates: using a ⅜-inch bit, drill in from the edges of the plates into the dowels. Glue ⅜-inch dowels in the holes; saw off the excess.

the dowels. Drill 1/16-inch pilot holes for the screws through the acrylic and 3/8 inch into the maple.

On the acrylic pieces only, drill through the 1/16-inch holes with a 7/64-inch bit. Smooth the cut edges of the acrylic with 400-grit wet and dry sandpaper. Attach the acrylic pieces to the maple pieces with woodscrews.

Insert the dowels through both end pieces. Sand the inside of the dowel holes and the dowels if there's any unnecessary binding.

Design: William Crosby.

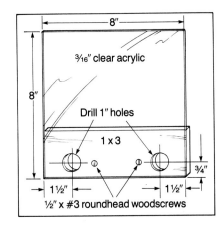

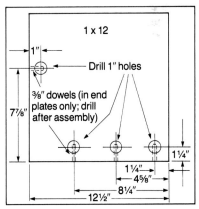

FURNITURE

ROLL-AROUND COMPUTER TABLE

This compact, movable table easily holds a personal computer. You can roll it up next to your desk or store it away, ready for occasional use.

If you wish, customize the table for your particular system by adding racks and shelves on top to fit the components. (If you have a detachable keyboard, you can also add a sliding shelf underneath.) You may want to adjust the table's height, too—to fit your own dimensions as well as those of your computer components. The customizing ideas shown at right should give you a good start in creating your own design.

Materials list

36″ by 25″ butcher block
9′ of 1½″ by 2½″ maple or birch
3′ of ¾″ by 7¼″ maple or birch
4′ of 1½″ by 7¼″ maple or birch
4 flathead woodscrews, 2½″ by #8
6 flathead Phillips screws, 2″ by #8, with
    finishing washers
20 flathead woodscrews, 1¼″ by #10
4 1¾″ stemmed casters
Wood putty
Polyurethane penetrating oil sealer
Glue

Cut lumber to dimensions given in drawing at right. Cut half-lap joints (see page 89) into the 1½-inch-thick uprights and supports as shown, using a power saw with a dado blade or a router. Then cut ¾ by 7¼-inch dadoes into the uprights for the cross brace.

Drill pilot holes in the uprights and bottom and top supports. Then glue and screw the pieces together, using 1¼-inch woodscrews. Drill pilot holes in the cross brace; glue and screw to the uprights, using 2-inch Phillips screws.

Place the top face down on a smooth surface (use a drop cloth to prevent scratches) and set the frame assembly on it. Counterbore ½-inch-wide, 1-inch-deep holes in the top supports. When supports are flush with front, back, and end edges of top and the assembly is square, drill pilot holes through the top supports and 1 inch into the top. Attach the frame to the top with 2½-inch woodscrews.

Drill holes for caster stems into the bottom supports; then insert the casters. Fill the screw holes with wood putty and sand the frame. Finally, apply a polyurethane penetrating oil sealer to the frame.

Design: Don Vandervort.

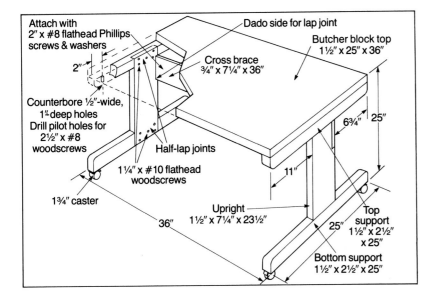

Attach with 2″ x #8 flathead Phillips screws & washers

2″

Counterbore ½″-wide, 1¼″-deep holes
Drill pilot holes for 2½″ x #8 woodscrews

1¾″ caster

1¼″ x #10 flathead woodscrews

Half-lap joints

36″

Dado side for lap joint

Cross brace ¾″ x 7¼″ x 36″

Butcher block top 1½″ x 25″ x 36″

25″

6¾″

11″

Upright 1½″ x 7¼″ x 23½″

25″

Top support 1½″ x 2½″ x 25″

Bottom support 1½″ x 2½″ x 25″

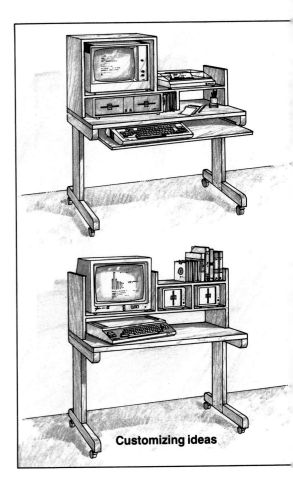

Customizing ideas

LAWN CHAIR

Comfort and classic styling make this lawn chair a welcome addition to your porch or back-yard furniture. We used redwood for our chair, but you can use any soft-wood species. Paint the finished chair, stain it, or let the natural wood color show through as we did. If you don't paint the chair, protect the wood with a nontoxic water-repellent preservative

Materials list

4' of 1 by 2
32' of 1 by 3: 4 @ 6'; 1 @ 8'
6' of 1 by 4
16' of 1 by 6: 2 @ 8'
1 box of galvanized flathead woodscrews,
    1¼" by #8
Waterproof glue
Finishing materials

Cut all pieces following the cutting list below.

A (2 arms): Two 1 by 6s @ 28½"*
B (2 arm supports): Two 1 by 6s @ 10½"*
C (2 support blocks): Two 1 by 3s @ 3½"
D (2 seat legs): Two 1 by 6s @ 31½"*
E (2 front legs): Two 1 by 4s @ 21"
F (1 front stretcher): One 1 by 4 @ 23"
G (2 tapering back splats): Ripped from
    one 1 by 3 @ 32"
H (1 center back splat): One 1 by 6 @ 35"
I (1 bottom cross brace): One 1 by 3 @ 20"
J (2 inside full splats): Two 1 by 3s @ 35"
K (2 outside full splats): Two 1 by 3s @ 34"
L (1 upper cross brace): One 1 by 2 @ 21"
M (1 middle cross brace): One 1 by
    2 @ 24"
N (1 back and leg brace): One 1 by
    3 @ 21½"
O (6 seat slats): Six 1 by 3s @ 21½"

* See grid patterns in Drawing 1.

Enlarge the grid patterns in Drawing 1, carefully transferring the patterns to the 1 by 6s for the arm pieces A and B and seat legs D. Cut two of each piece simultaneously, clamping the pairs securely so they don't shift. Round the back feet of the seat legs and the front corners and rear outside corners of the arms as shown.

Cut the remaining pieces. For the tapering outside back splats G, rip a 32-inch 1 by 3 so the two pieces are identical, measuring ½ inch at one end and 1⅞ inches at the other. Sand the edges.

As you assemble the chair, glue all connecting surfaces and secure each joint with screws to ensure that all joints stay locked together. Predrill and countersink all screw holes.

Start by assembling the H-shaped front support. In each front leg E, starting 10½ inches up from the bottom, cut a ¾-inch-deep by 3½-inch-long dado (see Drawing 2). The front stretcher F should sit flush in the dado. Attach the curved arm supports B so they are flush with the top and front edges of the legs; then attach the support blocks C flush with the tops of the legs behind the arm supports. Attach the stretcher F between the front legs.

Attach the seat legs D to the front legs so they butt against the back of the stretcher F and are flush with its top edge; be sure the front legs are vertical when the back legs touch the ground.

Next, assemble the back. Mount the center back splat H centered on top of the wide side of the 1 by 3 bottom cross brace I; place the splat so its bottom edge is flush with the bottom of the brace. Next, attach the

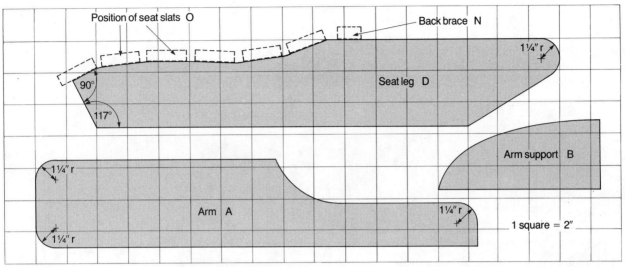

Position of seat slats O
Back brace N
1¼" r
Seat leg D
90°
117°
Arm support B
1¼" r
1¼" r
Arm A
1¼" r
1 square = 2"
1¼" r

Drawing 1

inside full splats J, one on each side of the center splat and each spaced ⅝ inch from it. Attach the outside full splats K ⅜ inch from the previous pair. Finally, use one screw to attach the ½-inch end of each of the tapering back splats G to the brace. Space the tapering splats ¼ inch from the adjacent splats, with their uncut edges facing inward.

Mount the upper cross brace L with its bottom edge 27½ inches up from the bottom of the back splats. Center the brace and attach with screws from the back; make sure spacing between splats remains even.

Rip a 30° bevel along the top edge of the middle cross brace M, which also supports the arms. Mount it centered on the back, with its bottom edge 15½ inches up from the bottom of the back splats and with the beveled edge up and facing toward the front of the chair.

Hold a string against the middle of the center splat 14 inches from the top. Using the string and a pencil as a compass, mark an arc across the top of the back; then cut the arc.

To attach the seat and back to each other, position the 1 by 3 back brace N on top of the seat legs as shown in Drawings 1 and 2; then attach it. Tuck the seat back's bottom cross brace I under this 1 by 3 and have someone hold the back steady while you set one screw on each side through the seat leg and into the cross brace. These will act as pivot points while you adjust the position of the arms and back.

Position the arms A so they overhang the arm supports B by 3 inches and the inner edges of the front legs by ¼ inch. Drive screws through the support blocks C and into the arms. Now adjust the back so the beveled side of cross brace M is flush with the arms; fasten the arms to the ends of the cross brace with single screws.

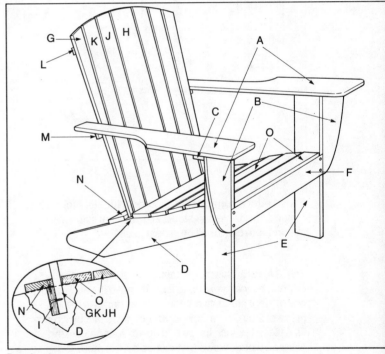

Drawing 2

Drive a second screw through each seat leg and into the cross brace I; then drive four screws through the back brace N into the cross brace I.

Finally, attach the six 1 by 3 seat slats O so the front edge of the first one is flush with the front of the stretcher. Leave ½-inch spaces between slats. Finish or paint your chair as desired; then sit down and relax!

Design: William Crosby.

COMPACT TABLE & STOOL SET

Styled after a compact set of outdoor furniture found in Finland, this table and stool set is an ideal solution to the problem of a small breakfast deck.

THE TABLE. This sturdy table is best suited for two people, but can seat up to four. To make it, you'll need one 10-foot piece, two 8-foot pieces, and one 6-foot piece of 2 by 4 hem-fir, one 10-foot piece of 4 by 4 hem-fir, 4 feet of ½-inch hardwood dowel, four galvanized flathead woodscrews (2½ inches by #8), and waterproof glue.

Cut eight 31-inch pieces of 2 by 4 for the tabletop (see Drawing 1). Drill ½-inch diameter, 1-inch-deep holes, centered 4 inches from each end, into the narrow sides of the 2 by 4s (drill only one side of the end pieces). Cut fourteen 2⅜-inch-long dowels and glue them into the holes; then assemble the tabletop, using pieces of ⅜-inch plywood as temporary spacers between the 2 by 4s.

Cut the 4 by 4 into four 26½-inch-long legs. Cut four 28-inch 2 by 4s for the top and bottom cross braces, cutting cross-lap joints as shown in Drawing 2 (see page 89 for cutting lap joints). Cut the ends of the two top cross braces back at a 45° angle. Drill holes for ½-inch dowels in one top and one bottom cross brace and assemble the pieces with glue. Also drill dowel holes 1¼ inches deep in one side of each leg (see Drawing 2) to match those in the crosspieces.

Cut four 3½-inch dowel pegs and insert them through the holes in the cross braces. Slide the legs onto the dowels, first coating all contacting surfaces with waterproof glue. Clamp in all directions, making sure everything is square and level before tightening the clamps. Glue the base to the top and fasten with woodscrews through the mitered ends of the cross braces.

After the glue is dry, sand the table and apply the finish of your choice.

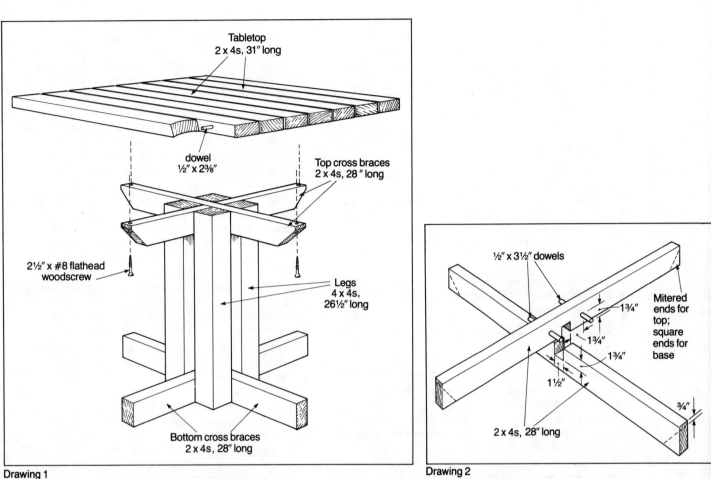

Tabletop
2 x 4s, 31″ long

dowel
½″ x 2⅜″

Top cross braces
2 x 4s, 28 ″ long

2½″ x #8 flathead
woodscrew

Legs
4 x 4s,
26½″ long

Bottom cross braces
2 x 4s, 28″ long

Drawing 1

½″ x 3½″ dowels

Mitered
ends for
top;
square
ends for
base

1¾″

1¾″

1¾″

1½″

¾″

2 x 4s, 28″ long

Drawing 2

THE STOOLS. To make two stools, you'll need four 8-foot pieces of 2 by 4 hem-fir, 6 feet of ½-inch hardwood dowel, 32 galvanized flathead woodscrews (2½ inches by #8), and waterproof glue.

For each stool, cut the 2 by 4s into twelve 15⅞-inch lengths, making 45° cuts at one end of the eight leg pieces and at both ends of the four top pieces. Drill two pilot holes horizontally into the top corners of each leg piece and countersink them for the woodscrews (see Drawing 3). Then glue and screw each piece to two leg pieces, making four U-shaped sections.

Drill ½-inch diameter holes, 1 inch deep, in the sides of the legs, centering the holes 4 inches and 14 inches down from the top. Cut twelve 2⅜-inch dowels, glue them into the holes, and assemble the sections, using pieces of ⅜-inch plywood for temporary spacers.

After the glue is dry, sand the stools and apply the finish of your choice.

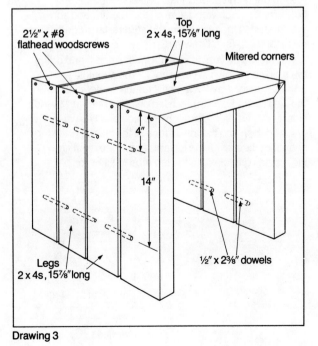

2½″ x #8
flathead woodscrews

Top
2 x 4s, 15⅞″ long

Mitered corners

4″

14″

Legs
2 x 4s, 15⅞″ long

½″ x 2⅜″ dowels

Drawing 3

FOLDING TABLES

Buffet-style entertaining is great for a crowd, but if you don't have enough sturdy eating surfaces, your guests may find dining a bit difficult. These folding tables—handsome enough to be part of your permanent décor—provide a solution to such problems. When you want them out of the way, just hang them up on their own wall-mounted rack.

Materials list

For 2 tables and 1 wall rack:
8' of 1" fir bull-nose stair tread
2' of 1 by 4 fir
28' of 1 by 2 fir: 2 @ 10', 1 @ 8'
9' of ¾" hardwood dowel: 3 @ 3' (be sure
  dowels are round and straight)
Scraps of ⅜" hardwood dowel
20 flathead woodscrews, 2½" by #12
8 flathead woodscrews, 1¼" by #10
8 small washers for #10 screws
3d (1¼") finishing nails
Glue
Satin-finish polyurethane (optional)

The stair tread measures about 11¼ inches wide. Rip it into 2 and 9-inch-wide pieces, making sure that the bull-nose is on the 9-inch-wide piece.

Cut the wider piece into four 23½-inch sections for the tabletops; cut four 16-inch cleats from the narrower piece. To make each tabletop, glue and clamp two of the 9-inch-wide pieces together, rounded edges out. Round each end of the cleats and drill countersunk holes for 2½-inch woodscrews; then center and screw the cleats 1½ inches in from the square-cut edges of each tabletop (see Drawing 2).

Cut the 1 by 2 legs to size, round the ends, and drill the holes as shown in Drawing 3. (You should have about 2 feet of 1 by 2 left; use it for the center piece of the wall rack.) Each 30-inch leg pivots around a 1¼-inch woodscrew running through one side and two washers, and then into the inside face of the cleats. Each leg should be flush with the top and end of the cleat, leaving a small gap close to the tabletop to allow for pivoting.

The 29¼-inch inside legs pivot around screws running through their centers and two washers, and then into the outer legs. Dowel crosspieces hold the inside legs rigid. Before cutting the dowel to size, screw the shorter (inside) and longer (outside) legs to one another and then to the cleats. Then measure the distance between the inside legs, from one outer edge to the other (approximately 16⅞ inches). Disassemble the legs; glue dowels into holes drilled in the inside legs. (Finishing nails help hold dowels in position.) Reassemble to check that inside and outside legs pivot freely.

At this point, you haven't done anything to stop the legs from folding, so the table will collapse instead of standing upright. Make stops for the legs from two pieces of ¾-inch dowel with shorter lengths of ⅜-inch dowel protruding ¾ inch, as shown in Drawing 1. These short dowels should align with the center of the top dowel crosspiece and slide into ⅜-inch holes drilled for them. To allow for the expected variations in your tables, make some test fittings to ensure that the tabletop is level before you glue the stops in place.

Disassemble the tables once again and sand all the surfaces; if you wish, apply several coats of a satin-finish polyurethane to the parts. Reassemble the tables when the finish is dry.

To build a wall rack to hold your tables, use the 1 by 4 for the back piece; cut the 14½-inch center piece from the extra 1 by 2. Round the ends and center the pieces (see Drawing 4); then glue and nail them together. Drill two holes for supporting dowels as shown in Drawing 4. Drill and countersink four holes for the 2½-inch woodscrews that hold the rack to the wall studs. Sand the rack; then finish it.

Design: Peter O. Whiteley.

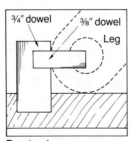

Drawing 1

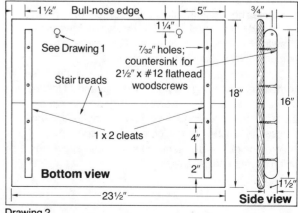

Drawing 2

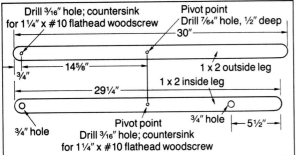

Drill ³⁄₁₆" hole; countersink
for 1¼" x #10 flathead woodscrew

Pivot point
Drill ⁷⁄₆₄" hole, ½" deep

30"

¾"

14⅝"

1 x 2 outside leg

29¼"

1 x 2 inside leg

¾" hole

Pivot point
Drill ³⁄₁₆" hole; countersink
for 1¼" x #10 flathead woodscrew

¾" hole

5½"

Drawing 3

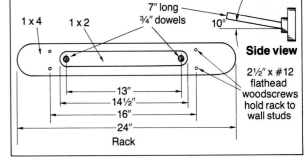

1 x 4

1 x 2

7" long
¾" dowels

10°

Side view

2½" x #12
flathead
woodscrews
hold rack to
wall studs

13"

14½"

16"

24"

Rack

Drawing 4

TILE-TOP TABLE

You'll find many uses for this easy-to-build table. Use it as a display stand for a favorite plant, or a side table alongside your patio chairs—and when you need extra outdoor seating, let it serve as a stool. If the tiles you choose don't match the size recommended below, you may have to alter the tabletop size to fit.

Materials list

12' of 1 by 4 clear heart redwood
6' of 1 by 3 clear heart redwood
6' of 1 by 1 redwood
16" by 16" piece of ½" exterior fir plywood
6d (2") galvanized finishing nails
3d (1¼") galvanized finishing nails
8 flathead galvanized woodscrews,
     1¼" by #10
32 glazed ceramic tiles, ¼" by 1⅞" by 3⅞"
Water-resistant mastic
Grout
Waterproof glue
Polyurethane penetrating oil sealer

Cut all pieces to the dimensions shown in the drawing. Round all edges of the legs and rails, using a router and a ¼-inch rounding bit (or use sandpaper).

Fasten the table rails together with glue and 2-inch finishing nails; predrill the ends of the long rails to prevent splitting. Make sure that all corners are square. Make each L-shaped leg by butting a 1 by 3 leg piece to a 1 by 4 leg piece (see drawing); glue and nail the legs, using 2-inch nails.

When the glue is dry, glue and nail the four 1 by 1 supports to the inside of the rails (as shown) using 1¼-inch finishing nails. Glue the legs to the rails, then screw together from the inside, as shown. Glue and nail the plywood to the supports, using 1¼-inch nails. Sand the wood, then apply sealer to all surfaces.

Spread mastic on the plywood and set the tiles in place, allowing ⅛-inch grout joints. Let the mastic set for 24 hours; then grout the tile joints according to the manufacturer's directions.

Design: Donald Rutherford.

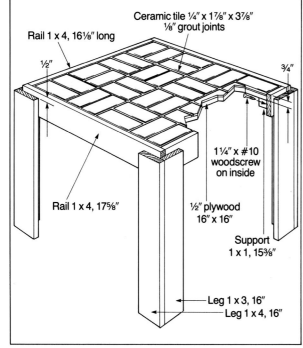

Ceramic tile ¼" x 1⅞" x 3⅞"
⅛" grout joints

Rail 1 x 4, 16⅛" long

½"

¾"

Rail 1 x 4, 17⅝"

1¼" x #10 woodscrew on inside

½" plywood 16" x 16"

Support 1 x 1, 15⅜"

Leg 1 x 3, 16"
Leg 1 x 4, 16"

BOLTED SQUARE TABLE

Contrasting woods and a simple, quickly assembled frame make this sturdy table both attractive and practical.

A table like this can be made any size; we tell you how to build one that's 29 inches high and 38 inches square. We recommend making the legs of redwood and the horizontal pieces of clear Douglas fir, all finished with a satin-finish polyurethane. (Of course, you can use other woods if you prefer.) The top is plywood covered with matte black plastic laminate.

Materials list

10′ of 4 by 4 redwood
12′ of 4 by 4 clear Douglas fir: 2 @ 6′
½ sheet of ⅝″ A-B fir plywood, 4′ by 4′
36″ square of 1/16″ matte black plastic
　　　laminate
Satin-finish polyurethane
16 ⅜″ by 4½″ hex-head bolts with nuts and
　　　washers
8 angle brackets

The frame consists of eight 4 by 4s (actually measuring 3½ by 3½ inches) bolted together. On a table saw, rip the 4 by 4s to form the two different L-shapes (see drawing); use redwood for the legs and fir for the horizontal pieces. Cut the legs 29 inches long and the horizontal pieces 31 inches long. To accentuate the intersections, cut 1/16 by 1/16-inch rabbets at the top and outside edges of the ends of the horizontal pieces.

Secure the hex-head bolts that hold the frame together with nuts and washers in holes drilled in the bottoms of the horizontal pieces. Since the bolts are slightly recessed, you'll need a socket wrench to tighten them. Wedge a screwdriver against the nuts in the holes to hold them in place while you're tightening the bolts.

Cut the plywood top ⅛ inch under size, to leave a 1/16-inch gap between the edges of the top (when centered) and the frame. Cover the top with the plastic laminate as recommended by the manufacturer. The top rests on the frame and is secured from underneath with two angle brackets on each side.

Design: Paul Smith.

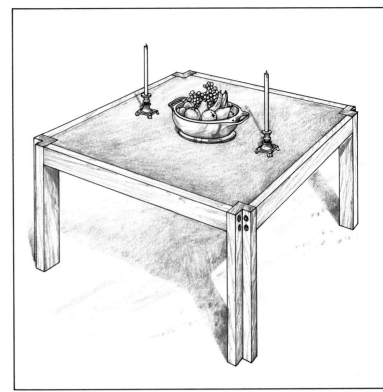

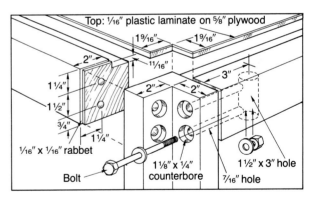

CANTILEVERED CHAIR

Elegantly streamlined, this cantilevered chair is sturdy, durable, and very comfortable. (For information on making cushions, see *Sunset*'s *Furniture Upholstery* or *How to Make Pillows*.)

Materials list

28′ of 1½″ by 1½″ birch
24″ by 24″ piece of ¼″ A-D fir plywood
16 flathead woodscrews, 1¼″ by #10
8 flathead woodscrews, 3″ by #12
14 panhead screws, 1¼″ by #10, with washers
1¼ yards of chair canvas, 45″ wide
White glue
1 cushion, 4″ by 25″ by 24″
1 cushion, 4″ by 16″ by 24″

Cut all pieces from 1½″ by 1½″ birch, following the cutting list below.

A (leg support): Two @ 33″
B (cross brace): Two @ 29″
C (front legs): Two @ 17″
D (back legs): Two @ 21″
E (frame ends): Two @ 28″
F (frame sides): Two @ 35½″

Cut the upper ends of pieces C and D at a 25° angle. From the plywood, cut two strips, each 1¼ by 20½ inches, to help fasten the seat sling to the frame; also cut a 22 by 20½-inch piece to support the seat.

Mark the placement of pieces A, C, D, and F; remember to cut and assemble the chair sides as mirror images of each other. Cut the joints on these pieces and on the ends of pieces B (see page 89). Also drill and counterbore pilot holes for all screws; you'll secure all joints with glue and screws as you assemble the chair.

Assemble the sides from pieces A, C, and D with glue and 1¼-inch flathead woodscrews, using a square to ensure that pieces C and D are perpendicular to A. While the glue dries, cut 1-inch-long open mortise and tenon joints on the ends of pieces E and F and assemble with glue and 3-inch woodscrews (see page 89). Glue and screw pieces B to the sides, using 3-inch woodscrews. Then glue and screw the sides to the seat frame, using 1¼-inch flathead woodscrews.

Plug the screw holes, using purchased plugs, plugs cut from birch scraps with a plug cutter, or dowels. Glue the plugs in place and sand them flush when the glue is dry. Sand the rest of the chair, rounding all edges. Apply the finish of your choice.

Fold canvas in half, right sides together. Stitch a ½-inch seam down the long edge; turn canvas right side out, keeping the seam as a side edge. Insert plywood at the bottom end of the fabric tube and fasten the sling to the chair with plywood strips and 1¼-inch panhead screws (see detail in upper left of drawing below).

Design adaptation: Paul Hamilton.

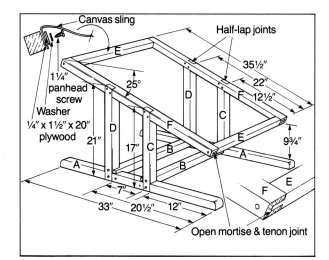

BUTCHER BLOCK TABLE

For a straightforward woodworking project, this butcher block table pays off with a lot of convenience: you get a good-size work surface, a shelf and pegs for pots and pans, and slots for knives and other utensils.

Materials list

25″ by 48″ maple butcher block, 1½″ thick
12′ of 4 by 4 Douglas fir: 2 @ 6′
24′ of 2 by 4 Douglas fir: 2 @ 6′, 3 @ 4′
12 lag screws, 4″ by ⅜″
10 flathead woodscrews, 3″ by #10
4 flathead woodscrews, 3″ by #12
6d (2″) finishing nails
3′ of ¼″ hardwood dowel
Polyurethane
Mineral oil

Starting with the butcher block, make three cuts off one long side to yield three 2⅜-inch-wide strips (this allows for ⅛-inch saw kerf). For tabletop rims, attach one strip on edge to each long side of the butcher block with three countersunk 3-inch by #10 woodscrews.

Cut the third butcher block strip into two 20½-inch lengths. Glue five small scraps of ½-inch-thick wood cut from block waste to each piece at regular intervals to function as knife spacers. Use 3-inch by #10 woodscrews to hold these knife-rack end rims and spacers to the butcher block tabletop.

Cut the legs from the 4 by 4s, making them 34½ inches long. Cut the 6-foot 2 by 4s into two 36-inch-long side braces and four 17½-inch-long end braces. The 4-foot 2 by 4s yield the three 42-inch-long shelf boards.

Use the lag screws to attach the side braces and two end braces to the tops of the legs. Attach the other two end braces a few inches from the bottom. Secure the shelf boards with nails. Attach the butcher block top with four countersunk 3-inch by #12 woodscrews driven horizontally through the long rims and into the legs.

To make pot hooks, cut the ¼-inch dowel into 2-inch lengths and glue into ¾-inch-deep holes drilled at a slight angle in the table's side braces.

Finish the base of the table with a polyurethane coating, and rub mineral oil over any surface that will come in contact with food.

Design: Jean Taylor.

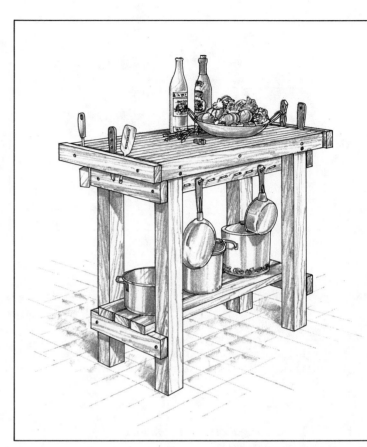

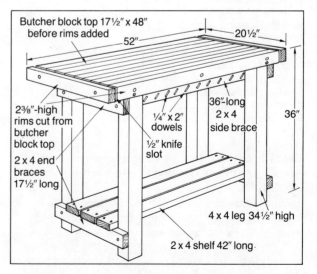

Butcher block top 17½″ x 48″ before rims added

52″

20½″

2⅜″-high rims cut from butcher block top

2 x 4 end braces 17½″ long

¼″ x 2″ dowels

½″ knife slot

36″-long 2 x 4 side brace

36″

4 x 4 leg 34½″ high

2 x 4 shelf 42″ long

GLASS-TOPPED TABLE

on legs where they intersect. Stack, rotate, and mark remaining two legs in the same way.

Cut off wood outside the top and bottom lines. Where the legs intersect, make a lap joint by routing out half the thickness of each piece (see page 89). Glue and clamp each set of legs and set aside to dry.

When the glue is dry, mark each leg for the mortise (see "Mortise and tenon joints," page 89). Use the nail hole as a center point and draw a ¾ by 2¾-inch box around it. Drill out the square with a ¾-inch bit. Use a sharp chisel or saber saw to square the hole after drilling.

To make the tenons on the bottom rail, draw a line on all four sides of the 60-inch 2 by 4, 1½ inches from each end. Next, draw a ¾ by 2¾-inch rectangle centered on each end. Extend the lines of this rectangle down the sides to the lines you already marked on the rail. Use the lines as guides to cut the tenons; fit the tenons carefully to the mortises.

Now rip each of the 2 by 6 side rails on both edges at an angle to match the tops of the legs. Cut the two 2 by 4 crosspieces to size, mitering the ends at the same angle as the sides of the legs.

Clamp the crosspieces to the tops of the legs, drill ⅜-inch dowel holes, and glue all in place (see drawing below). When the glue is dry, square and clamp the side rails to the crosspieces and drill two dowel holes in the overlapping ends of each side rail and crosspiece. Insert the bottom rail into each leg assembly and dry-dowel the side rails (do not glue). Drill dowel holes in the legs through the tenons.

Dismantle the side and bottom rails and apply glue to all joints; then reassemble (bottom rail first, then side rails) and clamp. When the glue is dry, fill gaps with wood putty; then sand the entire table and apply the finish of your choice. Add the glass top and your table is complete.

Design: Bill Black.

This glass-topped table adds a touch of beauty to a patio setting, yet it won't dominate its surroundings. Use it outdoors or indoors as a dining or buffet table.

Some careful joinery—disguised from view—gives the table exceptional strength and stability. Be sure to make the joints accurately and with care.

Materials list

Lumber should be clear redwood or equivalent.
For a 2′ by 5′ table:
26′ of 2 by 4: 1 @ 10′, 2 @ 8′
10′ of 2 by 6: 1 @ 10′
16 ⅜″ hardwood dowels, 2½″
2 16d (3½″) nails
24″ by 60″ sheet of ½″ clear plate glass, polished edges
Waterproof glue
Wood putty

Cut all pieces to length. You'll need one 60-inch, four 42-inch, and two 21-inch-long 2 by 4s, and two 57-inch-long 2 by 6s.

Mark the centers of the 42-inch 2 by 4 legs on the wide faces and drill a ⅛-inch hole through each center mark. Stack two of the legs and put a 3½-inch nail through the holes. Rotate the top leg until the outer corners of the two legs are 24 inches apart at one end (see drawing at right); clamp the legs together.

Place a board across legs so that top edge of board is level with top two outer corners of legs; draw a straight line across the two legs. Measure down 32 inches, place board across bottom ends of legs, and mark another line (see drawing at right). Also draw lines

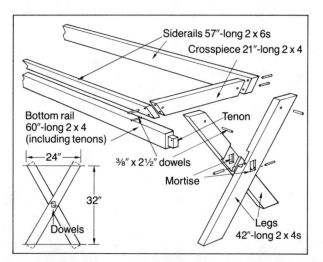

Siderails 57″-long 2 x 6s
Crosspiece 21″-long 2 x 4
Bottom rail 60″-long 2 x 4 (including tenons)
Tenon
⅜″ x 2½″ dowels
Mortise
24″
32″
Dowels
Legs 42″-long 2 x 4s

TROMPE L'OEIL COFFEE TABLE

In French, *trompe l'oeil* means "trick the eye"—and that's just what this coffee table does. Attractive paneling covers a simple particle board frame to make a table that's a lot less expensive than it appears.

For the paneling, use 3/16 by 3½-inch all-heart redwood or cedar strips with one smooth side. These are sold in packages at hardware stores and lumberyards. Other thin materials, such as plywood, oak flooring, and wood veneer, are also suitable.

Materials list

For 1 coffee table approximately 2' by 5':
96' of redwood or cedar paneling strips,
   3/16" by 3½": 12 @ 8'
1 sheet of ¾" particle board, 4' by 8'
20' of ⅜" by 2¼" redwood or cedar batten:
   2 @ 6', 1 @ 8'
18" of 4 by 4 redwood or cedar, or 8 13" angle
   brackets
40 flathead woodscrews, 2½" by #10
4d (1½") finishing nails
Powdered plastic resin glue
Contact cement
Wood putty
Polyurethane penetrating oil sealer
Varnish or polyurethane

To make the table, cut the sheet of particle board to the dimensions shown in Drawing 1. Then, using a powdered plastic resin glue, glue together the two top pieces and the two pairs of end pieces to create a double thickness. Keep the ¾-inch overlap for the rabbet joints (see Drawing 2). Clamp the pieces together overnight.

Now glue the three pieces together, making sure the corners are square, and set woodscrews through the joints 3 inches apart (see inset of Drawing 2). To further strengthen the table, block the joints as shown. You can make the blocks from an 18-inch piece of 4 by 4 ripped in half diagonally. (You can use other materials, such as metal angle brackets, in place of the 4 x 4.) Glue and screw the blocks (or brackets) into place at least 3 inches in from the edges. Use six screws for each block.

The redwood paneling strips come with beveled edges. To get tighter seams, rip off the bevel so the final width of each strip is 3 inches (eight rows span the table perfectly). Miter the ends of the strips where they meet at the outside corners. Cut the strips with special care to ensure a snug fit.

After you've cut all the strips, cover the table and the backs of the strips with contact cement and set strips in place. To guarantee a good bond, use a brayer to push

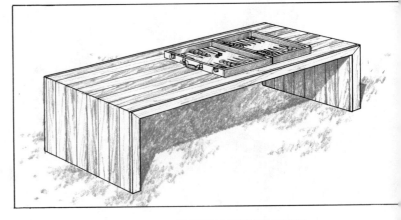

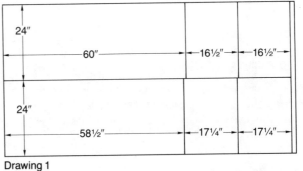

Drawing 1

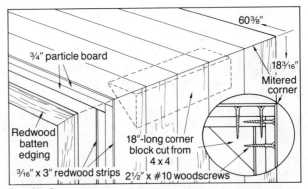

Drawing 2

the strips down. Keep the outside strips flush with the edge of the particle board; sand edges, if necessary.

Use ⅜ by 2¼-inch batten to cover the outside edge. Cut the width of the batten to the thickness of the table edge. Miter the batten corners, contact-cement the battens to the table, and reinforce with finishing nails. Fill nail holes and any cracks with putty that matches the color of the wood. Sand all surfaces smooth and round all sharp corners.

To finish the table, first harden the wood with two or three coats of a polyurethane penetrating oil sealer, then finish with varnish or polyurethane.

PATIO TABLE

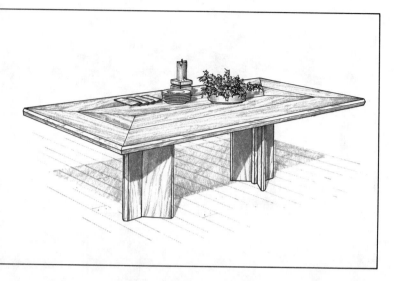

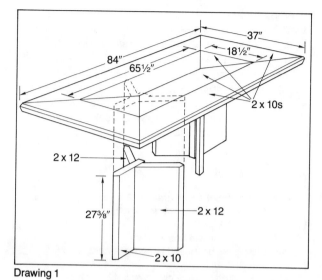

Drawing 1

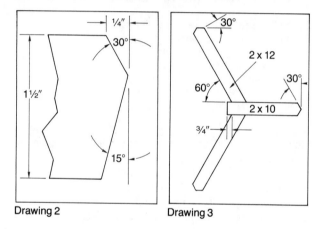

Drawing 2   Drawing 3

Sturdy yet portable, this outdoor table seats eight for dining and performs equally well as a buffet. The tabletop and pedestal bases are made entirely of surfaced 2 by 10 and 2 by 12 stock.

Materials list

**Lumber should be redwood or cedar for
    outdoor use.
For a 37″ by 7′ table:
42′ of 2 by 10: 1 @ 10′, 4 @ 8′
10′ of 2 by 12
8d (2½″) galvanized finishing nails
Waterproof glue
About 50 ⅜″ hardwood dowels, 2½″ long
Nontoxic, water-repellent wood preservative
    (optional)**

To form the top, cut the eight pieces as shown in Drawing 1. Cut the 84-inch and 65½-inch pieces from the 8-foot 2 by 10s; cut the remaining pieces from the 10-foot 2 by 10. Bevel the outer edges of the 84-inch and 37-inch pieces as shown in Drawing 2. Lightly sand all the surfaces with fine sandpaper before assembling the tabletop. Assemble the tabletop using blind dowel joints; space the dowels 6 inches apart (see "Reinforcement," page 90). Use waterproof glue on the diagonal joints only.

To make the bases, cut two pieces 27⅜ inches long, one each from the remainder of the 8-foot 2 by 10s. Next, cut four 27⅜-inch-long pieces from the 10-foot 2 by 12. Make 60° cuts on these four pieces as shown in Drawing 3. Then finish all six pieces with 30° bevels

at their outer ends. Assemble each pedestal using waterproof glue and galvanized finishing nails.

Turn the top of the table upside down and attach the pedestals, using blind dowels with glue. Let the glue dry before turning the table upright.

The diagonal pattern of the tabletop enhances the appearance of the wood grain. You can leave the table unpainted and unvarnished and enjoy the wood's natural beauty—or, if you wish, give your table a warm buckskin color by applying two coats of a nontoxic, water-repellent wood preservative. As the wood weathers, the color will gradually take on a grayish tinge; reapply preservative as necessary to retain the buckskin shade.

Design: Mark Mills.

TRESTLE TABLE

This handsome trestle table is one version of a classic European design that's several centuries old. Use the table for dining or for an extra-large desk or work table.

A project of this scope requires some woodworking expertise. If you don't have much experience, practice making the sliding dovetail and mortise and tenon joints used in the table's construction before you build.

Materials list

42' of 3 by 6 pine or fir: 3 @ 12', 1 @ 6'
36' of 2 by 6 pine or fir: 6 @ 6'
18' of 2 by 3 pine or fir: 3 @ 6'
3' of ½ by 4 pine or fir
15 flathead woodscrews, 2½" by #10
3 flathead woodscrews, 1½" by #8
6' of 4 by 4 pine or fir (mill down to 3" by 3"
     with square corners)
Glue

To remove the rounded edges and to true the edges for gluing, the 2 by 6s and 3 by 6s for the end panels and the top must be cut down to a width of 5 inches. A woodworking shop or mill will do this job for you. If you prefer to do it yourself, use a power saw or jointer; or do it by hand with a jointer plane.

First, glue together seven 3 by 6s, each 6 feet long, for the top, and five 2 by 6s, each 3 feet long, for each end panel. You'll need at least six bar or pipe clamps with capacities of 3 feet or more. Before you apply glue, test each joint to make sure it fits properly; if it doesn't, use a plane or sandpaper to make the necessary adjustments. Apply glue sparingly (remove any excess after glue is dry) and clamp the boards together, one joint at a time. Make the top faces of the boards as flush as possible and true them with a plane or sandpaper, if needed, before proceeding to the next joint.

After the glue of the last joint is dry, trim the top to length and round the top edges with a router and a ¼-inch rounding bit. (All rounded edges are cut with a ¼-inch bit unless otherwise noted.) Cut the end panels to length (26½ inches); then cut the angled sides and round the edges (see Drawing 1). Cut the bottom tenons. Finally, lay out and cut the mortises (see page 89).

While the glue of the top and end panel joints is drying, you can make the two feet (see Drawing 2 on page 36). It's easiest to cut the curved profile with a bandsaw. If you don't have access to one, first rough out the shape with a radial-arm, table, or saber saw; then do the final shaping with wood rasps, files, and sandpaper. Lay out the mortises and cut them to make a sliding fit with the end panel tenons. Round off the edges indicated. Cut four 3½ by 8-inch pads for the feet from the ½ by 4, rounding all the long edges.

(Continued on page 36)

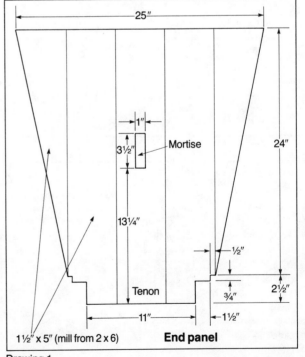

Drawing 1

Cut-away section

18"

14"

5½"

¾" Mortise

1½"

1½" 2½"

2"

Round edges, ¼"r

29"

½" r

½" r

1"

3"

3"

7½"

Cut from 4 x 4

Foot

Drawing 2

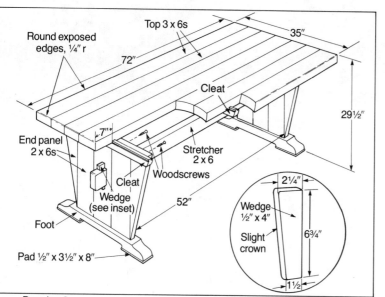

Round exposed
edges, ¼" r

Top 3 x 6s

35"

72"

Cleat

29½"

End panel
2 x 6s

7"

Stretcher
2 x 6

Woodscrews

Cleat

52"

Wedge
(see inset)

Foot

Pad ½" x 3½" x 8"

Wedge
½" x 4"

Slight
crown

2¼"

6¾"

1½"

Drawing 3

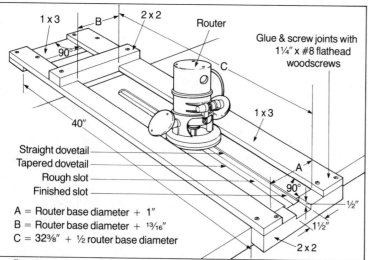

1 x 3

B

2 x 2

Router

90°

40"

Glue & screw joints with
1¼" x #8 flathead
woodscrews

C

1 x 3

A

90°

Straight dovetail
Tapered dovetail
Rough slot
Finished slot

½"

1½"

A = Router base diameter + 1"
B = Router base diameter + 13/16"
C = 32⅜" + ½ router base diameter

2 x 2

Drawing 4

On the underside of the tabletop, mark the locations of the cleats and end panels (see Drawing 3). True up the areas with a plane, and sandpaper them to make them absolutely flat. The sliding dovetail joints connecting the cleats to the top have one side tapered ¹⁄₁₆ inch per foot for ease of assembly. This is easily accomplished with a router, a ½-inch dovetail bit, and the simple jigs illustrated in Drawings 4 and 5. If you don't want to tackle the dovetails, you can secure the cleats to the top with 3-inch by #10 roundhead woodscrews and ³⁄₁₆-inch washers. In each cleat, counterbore five equally-spaced ¾-inch holes, 1 inch deep. Then drill ⅜-inch holes through. These oversized holes allow for the contraction and expansion of the top.

Re-mark the locations of the three cleats with parallel lines running across the underside of the tabletop. These also mark the root or widest part of the dovetail. Build the jig illustrated in Drawing 4 and clamp it to the underside of the tabletop, lining up the notch in the 2 by 2 with the marks for a cleat and placing the 2 by 2 tight against the top. Since the dovetail slot and tongues must be cut with only one depth setting of the router bit, remove as much of the waste as possible with a ¼-inch straight bit. Set the depth at slightly less than the finished depth. Repeat for the other two slots.

Replace the straight bit with the dovetail bit and adjust it to make a ½-inch-deep cut. Do not change this setting until you have cut all the dovetail slots and tongues. Still using the jig, finish routing the slots.

Cut the 2 by 3s into six 35-inch pieces: three for cleats, one for a test piece, and two for help in guiding the router when you cut the dovetail tongues in the cleats. Cut ½ by ½-inch rabbets in the guides (see Drawing 5). Do this either with a power saw or with the router *before* you set the depth on the dovetail bit. Cut a piece of wood about 1 inch wide, 2 inches long, and exactly ³⁄₁₆ inch thick for a shim to assure that the taper of the tongues exactly matches the slots in the tabletop.

Clamp the test piece between the two guides with the shim in place as shown. Clamp only at the ends, making sure the tops of all three pieces are flush. Nail some wood scraps to your work surface to keep the clamped pieces in place while you're routing the tongue. Adjust the edge guide to make the widest possible cut at the front of the right side of the piece. Rout the tapered (right) side of the test piece and then the three cleats.

Clamp the test piece between the guides again, but without the shim. Readjust the router edge guide to make slightly less than a full cut; make a pass on the left side. Cut off ⅝ inch of the dovetail tongue at the narrow end.

To assure a perfect fit of the tongue in the dovetail, remove the remaining material in small increments, testing after each cut. Be patient—this takes time. You'll have a proper fit when $\frac{1}{32}$ to $\frac{1}{16}$ inch of the wide end projects beyond the tabletop edge. Without touching the edge guide adjustment, complete the tongues of the three cleats and notch the narrow ends.

Cut the three cleats to 31 inches long, cutting off the wide ends. Save the cut-off portion for plugs to close the open ends of the slots. Angle the ends of the cleats and round off the edges (see Drawing 6). Wax the tongues and slide them into the slots, tapping the ends with a soft-headed mallet to seat them.

Cut dovetail plugs from the ends cut from the cleats. If you want to be able to dismantle the table, secure the plugs in the two end slots with $1\frac{1}{2}$-inch woodscrews; otherwise, simply glue them in place. Sand the plugs flush and round off the bottom edges of the top.

Check the shoulder-to-shoulder distance between the stretcher tenons by clamping the end panels to the cleats and measuring the distance between them. Cut the 2 by 6 for the stretcher 62 inches long; then cut the tenons (see Drawing 7 and pages 89–90) to slide easily into the end panel mortises. Cut the tapered wedges from the $\frac{1}{2}$ by 4 (see inset of Drawing 3). Now cut the mortise in each of the tenons so the wedge slides easily on the wide faces. Round off the edges of the stretchers; also round the ends of the tenons at a $\frac{1}{2}$-inch radius as shown.

You'll find it much easier to finish the table if you do the finishing before final assembly. Clean and finish sand all pieces; then mask all gluing surfaces with masking tape. Apply the finish of your choice.

After the finish is dry, assemble the table upside down. Glue, clamp, and screw one panel to a cleat as shown in Drawing 6, using $2\frac{1}{2}$-inch woodscrews. Insert the stretcher tenons into the mortises of both end panels; make sure that the wide ends of the mortises in the tenons face the tabletop. Then glue, clamp, and screw the other end panel to its cleat. Tap the wedges into the stretcher mortises until the tenon shoulders are tight against the panels.

Glue the feet to the end panels, making sure they're fully seated. Glue and screw the pads to the feet with $1\frac{1}{2}$-inch woodscrews, drilling pilot holes and countersinking the heads at least $\frac{1}{8}$ inch. If you plan to place the table on a wood floor, fill the screw holes with wood putty, and glue felt to the bottoms of the pads.

Design: Herman Novak.

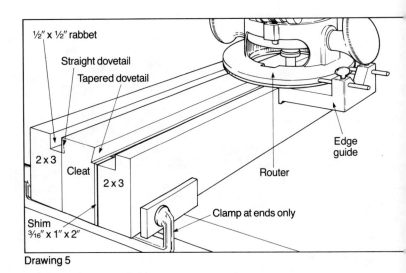

Drawing 5

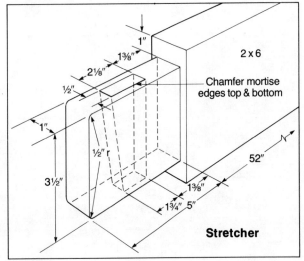

Drawing 6

Drawing 7

STORAGE BED

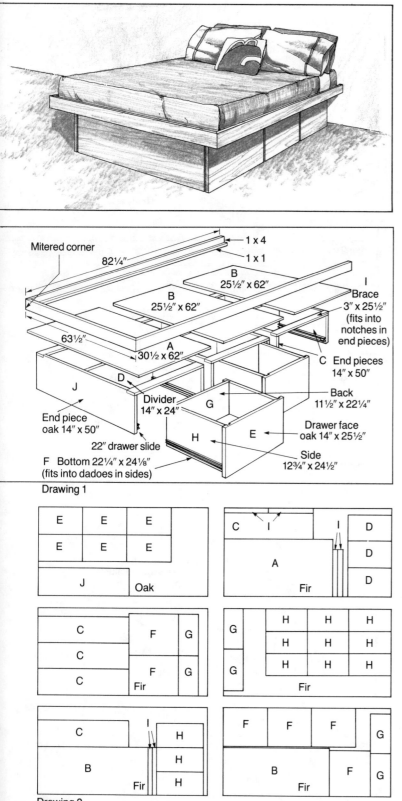

Drawing 1

Mitered corner
82¼″
1 x 4
1 x 1
B
25½″ x 62″
B
25½″ x 62″
I
Brace
3″ x 25½″
(fits into notches in end pieces)
63½″
A
30½″ x 62″
C End pieces
14″ x 50″
J
D
Divider
14″ x 24″
G
Back
11½″ x 22¼″
End piece
oak 14″ x 50″
22″ drawer slide
Drawer face
oak 14″ x 25½″
F Bottom 22¼″ x 24⅛″
(fits into dadoes in sides)
H
E
Side
12¾″ x 24½″

Drawing 2

Three modular units, each equipped with two roomy storage drawers, make the base of this platform bed. A 1 by 4 rim screwed to the platform tops of the units holds everything in place. The completed bed fits a queen-size mattress, with room for tucked-under bedding.

Materials list

To fit a 60″ by 80″ queen-size mattress:
5 sheets of ¾″ fir plywood, 4′ by 8′
1 sheet of ¾″ oak veneer plywood, 4′ by 8′
22′ of 1 by 4 oak: 2 @ 8′, 1 @ 6′
22′ of 1 by 1 oak: 2 @ 8′, 1 @ 6′
24 angle brackets
6 sets of heavy-duty, full-extension drawer slides, ½″ by 22″ long
60 flathead woodscrews, 1¼″ by #8
Glue
6d (2″) finishing nails
Veneer tape (optional)

Cut fir and oak plywood pieces according to the layouts in Drawing 2, allowing a ⅛-inch saw kerf when laying out cuts on plywood. Make trial fittings whenever possible.

To make each double-drawer unit strong, fasten a center divider D to the two end pieces C (to C and J for the unit at the foot of the bed) with eight angle brackets, and glue and nail 3-inch-wide plywood braces I into notches cut into each top corner.

Glue the drawer pieces together. The backs and bottoms fit in ¾-inch-wide, ⅜-inch-deep dadoes in the sides H, ½ inch from the edges; the sides fit in similar dadoes 1¼ inches from the drawer face E edges. (Before gluing, check fit by assembling all pieces in a dry run.) Drawer-face edges that will show at the foot of the bed can be covered with a glued strip of oak veneer cut away from the plywood (use veneer tape if you prefer).

After the drawers and slides are mounted, nail the platforms A and B in place. Trim and sand adjacent drawer edges, if necessary, to allow at least ¹⁄₁₆-inch clearance between faces when the drawer units are in position.

Glue and screw oak 1 by 1s to the inside of each 1 by 4 rim, ¾ inch from the lower edge; then screw the rim from above through the 1 by 1s into platform pieces A and B. Space all screws approximately 8 inches apart.

Design: Mary Ord.

BUNK BEDS

When space is at a premium, bunk beds can save the day. These simple and sturdy frames were designed with stacking in mind—but they can stand alone, too.

You can choose any species of wood to make the frames; one good selection is premium-grade clear kiln-dried redwood. Though it's on the expensive side, it's practical: very little finishing work is required.

Materials list

For 1 single bed:
12′ of 4 by 4
24′ of 2 by 6: 3 @ 8′
8′ of 1 by 6
18″ of ¾″ hardwood dowel
16″ of ⅜″ hardwood dowel (optional)
16 machine bolts, ¼″ by 2½″, with washers
         and nuts
8 machine bolts, ¼″ by 3½″, with washers
         and nuts
Glue
Polyurethane penetrating oil sealer
39″ by 75″ bolt-on steel-framed flat link
         springs (primarily used for bunk beds)

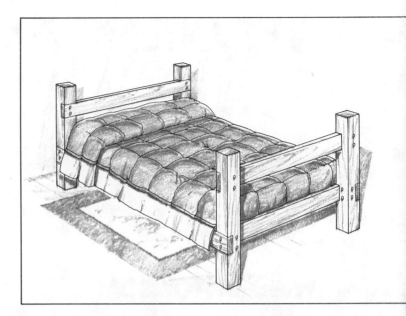

Cut the wood to length according to the dimensions in the drawing at right. Then mark and dado the posts to receive the 1 by 6 and 2 by 6 rails. For the cleanest results, use a radial-arm or table saw to make the dado cuts (see "Dado joints," page 88). If you use hand tools, mark the dimension of the dadoes on each post with a square; then carefully make the side cuts with a back-saw. Score the bottom lines of the dadoes with a large wood chisel and remove the wood between the cuts using the chisel.

To recess the bolts, drill ¾-inch-diameter holes about ¾ inch deep in the exposed faces of the 2 by 6s and 4 by 4s (don't counterbore the 1 by 6s). Then drill ¼-inch holes through for the bolts. Bolt the frame together, using the 3½-inch bolts to attach the flat link springs.

Dress up the frame with dowel plugs, or leave it un-plugged for easy knockdown. To plug the holes, insert a dowel into each hole and mark cutoff line flush with surface. Remove dowel, cut to length, line the hole with glue, and insert the cut piece.

Sand surfaces smooth and apply two coats of poly-urethane penetrating oil sealer (you can easily touch this up if the wood gets marred). If you want to stack the beds, drill ⅜-inch-diameter holes 2 inches deep in the tops of one bed's posts and the bottoms of the other bed's posts. Insert a 4-inch-long ⅜-inch dowel in each post of the bottom bed; then stack the other bed on it. The dowels keep the beds in position.

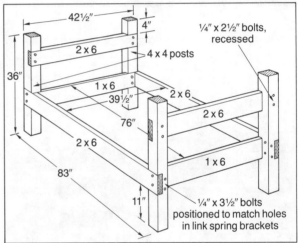

CHILDREN'S FURNITURE & TOYS

WIND-UP TOY BOAT

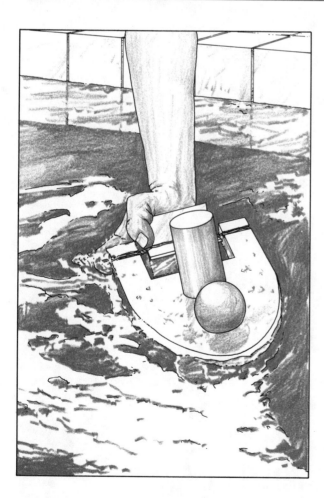

The simple pleasures of a bygone era return with this rubber-band-powered boat.

To make your own paddlewheel boat, you'll need a 9-inch piece of 1 by 6 pine for the hull, 5 inches of ¼ by 2¼-inch lattice for the wheel, a wooden drawer pull, and a piece of closet pole for the smokestack.

Enlarge the pattern pieces in the drawing below; then cut out the pieces, using a coping saw or jigsaw. Notch the prongs on the hull with a sharp knife or saw. Round and smooth sharp corners on the paddlewheel blades with sandpaper.

Fit the two paddlewheel blades together and glue them with epoxy glue. Next, attach the drawer pull and closet pole to the hull with epoxy. Waterproof the boat with two or three coats of a polyurethane finish or an oil-base enamel. Stretch a heavy rubber band across the prongs on the hull, positioning it in the shallow notches. Then tuck the paddlewheel in between the top and bottom of the rubber band.

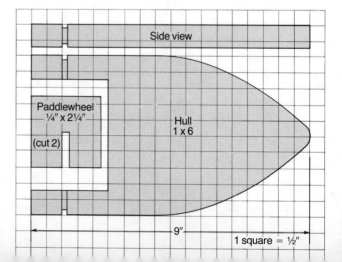

Side view

Paddlewheel
¼" x 2¼"

(cut 2)

Hull
1 x 6

9"

1 square = ½"

MURAL WORK TABLE

This mural table is just the right place for your "pre-school Picassos" to express themselves with paints, crayons, or stamp pads. Paper pulls out to mural size from a large roll at the end of the table; plastic tubs below provide washable storage space for messy paints.

Materials list

1 hollow-core door, 24" by 80"
16' of 1 by 4 clear fir: 2 @ 8'
24' of 1 by 2 clear fir: 4 @ 6'
22' of 1 by 1 clear fir: 2 @ 8', 1 @ 6'
2' of ¼" by 1¼" lattice
3' of ⅞" hardwood dowel
9' of ¼" hardwood dowel
Glue
4 plastic dish tubs
1 roll of paper
Polyurethane penetrating oil sealer
Clear polyurethane exterior finish

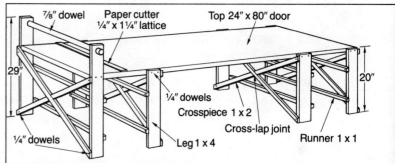

Cut one 29-inch leg and three 20-inch legs from each 1 by 4. Drill a hole for the 27-inch-long dowel in one end of each 29-inch leg. This dowel will hold the paper roll, so be sure you position it high enough to let the roll turn easily.

The distance between the legs is determined by the width of the plastic dish tubs you select. Calculate the spacing between the legs by measuring the tub's width just below its lip, then adding the width of the runners which will be attached to the legs along both sides of the tub. (Tubs should slide freely, so allow some leeway between runners and tub sides.)

After you've determined the leg spacing, use a square to make sure the angle of leg to table surface is 90°. Then drill pairs of ¼-inch holes, 2 inches deep and 2 inches apart, through each leg and into the edge of the door (which forms the tabletop). Add glue and insert ¼-inch dowels (about 2⅛ inches long).

The crosspieces provide lateral strength. Make them from the 1 by 2s. Cut the first crosspiece so that it reaches from the bottom of one leg to the point where the opposite leg meets the tabletop (see drawing at right). Use this crosspiece as a pattern for cutting the remaining seven crosspieces.

Cut a dado halfway through each of the crosspieces where they cross so outer surfaces are flush when the boards are joined (see "Dado joints" and "Lap joints" on pages 88–89). To cut dadoes, make several cuts halfway through with a saw; then chisel out the wood

between the cuts. Attach the crosspieces to the table legs with glue and ¼-inch dowels. When the glue is dry, saw off protruding ends of crosspieces flush with the table legs.

From the 1 by 1s, cut 25½-inch runners to span the legs; glue and dowel them in place. To make a paper cutter, glue and dowel the ends of the lattice to the top of the table.

To finish, sand the table thoroughly, making sure all dowels are flush, and round all corners for safety. For a hard, easily cleaned surface, coat the table with a polyurethane penetrating oil sealer. When sealer is dry, apply three coats of a polyurethane exterior finish.

Design: Marylee MacDonald.

SMALL FRY'S DESK

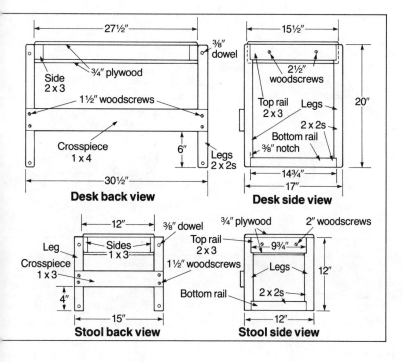

Desk back view
- 27½"
- ⅜" dowel
- ¾" plywood
- Side 2 x 3
- 1½" woodscrews
- Crosspiece 1 x 4
- 6"
- Legs 2 x 2s
- 30½"

Desk side view
- 15½"
- 2½" woodscrews
- Top rail 2 x 3
- Legs
- 2 x 2s
- Bottom rail
- ⅜" notch
- 20"
- 14¾"
- 17"

Stool back view
- 12"
- ⅜" dowel
- Leg
- Sides 1 x 3
- Crosspiece 1 x 3
- 4"
- 15"

Stool side view
- ¾" plywood
- 2" woodscrews
- Top rail 2 x 3
- 9¾"
- 1½" woodscrews
- Legs
- Bottom rail
- 2 x 2s
- 12"
- 12"

This pint-size desk with stool is the perfect project for woodworkers who don't have much time to spare. Cut and glue the legs and tops one day; screw them together the next day. Sand and seal the desk and stool the day after that.

You need only basic woodworking skills to build these—the most difficult cuts are the ⅜-inch notches made in the legs. The rest are straight crosscuts.

Materials list

For 1 desk and 1 stool:
16′ of 2 by 2 birch: 2 @ 8′
8′ of 2 by 3 birch
3′ of 1 by 4 birch
4′ of 1 by 3 birch
½ sheet of ¾″ birch plywood, 4′ by 4′
3′ of ⅜″ hardwood dowel
8 flathead woodscrews, 1½″ by #8
4 flathead woodscrews, 2″ by #8
4 flathead woodscrews, 2½″ by #12
3d (1¼″) finishing nails
Glue
Wood putty
Clear finish
Oak legal-size letter tray (optional)

Start by cutting the wood to size.

Desk legs: Four 2 by 2s @ 20″
Desk top rails: Two 2 by 3s @ 14¾″
Desk bottom rails: Two 2 by 2s @ 14¾″
Desk crosspiece: One 1 by 4 @ 30½″
Desk sides: Two 2 by 3s @ 15½″
Stool legs: Four 2 by 2s @ 12″
Stool top rails: Two 2 by 3s @ 9¾″
Stool bottom rails: Two 2 by 2s @ 9¾″
Stool crosspiece: One 1 by 3 @ 15″
Stool side pieces: Two 1 by 3s @ 12″

Notch the vertical 2 by 2s for the desk and stool legs to receive the 2 by 3 and 2 by 2 top and bottom rails (see "Rabbet joints, page 88). Then center and mark the locations for the dowel holes in the sides of the legs opposite the notches (see "Reinforcement," page 90). Glue and clamp the verticals and rails together; then, using a ⅜-inch bit, drill 2-inch-deep holes at the marked points. Put glue in the holes, then hammer in 2¼-inch-long pieces of dowel. After the glue is dry, trim off the dowel ends and sand smooth. Cut the 1 by 4 and 1 by 3 crosspieces to size. (These keep the legs spread apart and prevent side-to-side movement.)

To assemble the open desk top, glue and nail two 15½ by 27½-inch pieces of plywood to the 2 by 3 side

pieces. Drill small pilot holes to make driving the nails easier. Make the stool top by gluing and nailing two 12 by 12-inch plywood pieces to the two 12-inch-long 1 by 3 side pieces. Countersink all nails and fill holes with wood putty.

If you want a permanent bond, glue and screw all joints when you assemble the desk top, legs, and crosspiece. If you want to be able to take the desk apart later, just use four 1½-inch and four 2½-inch wood-screws. Drill and countersink pilot holes for all screws.

Use 2-inch woodscrews and glue to join the stool top to its legs; drive the screws through the 2 by 3s of the

side into the 1 by 3s of the top. Then glue and screw on the crosspiece, using four 1½-inch woodscrews. Sand all surfaces and apply the finish.

For storing crayons, pencils, and other small objects, you can purchase an oak letter tray that holds legal-size paper. A 2⅜-inch-high tray (usually available in stationery stores) fits perfectly into the desk top.

Design: Gary Foltz of Williams and Foltz.

HORSE SWING

Whooshing through the air on a swing is one of life's great delights. And making this swing is a delight, too— all you need are a few pieces of wood, some rope, and a place to hang it. Best of all, you need only a few hours' time.

This flying horse swing is an updated version of an old playground standby: the three-rope, push-pull animal. Kids find the swinging horse fun to ride and dream on, and grownups like the way it teaches children coordination—how to use arms and legs for propulsion.

Materials list

Lumber should be construction-grade Douglas fir or equivalent. Choose wood that's free of large or loose knots.
8' of 2 by 4
2' of 2 by 12
30" of ¾" hardwood dowel
18" of 1" hardwood dowel
8 washers, 1" holes
6d (2") finishing nails
2 flathead woodscrews, 3" by #12
Waterproof glue
⅜" rope
Clear, nontoxic wood preservative

From the 2 by 4, cut out the legs and body as indicated in Drawing 1; round the ends. Also cut out a round spacer block. Cut out the head and saddle from the 2 by 12 (see Drawing 2).

The horse's head and legs pivot on a ¾-inch dowel through an oversize (1-inch) hole in the body. Washers on dowels keep adjacent parts evenly spaced, and they protect the wood from rubbing at the pivot point.

Position head and spacer block between legs; then clamp pieces together. Drill ¾-inch holes through all thicknesses, as indicated; also drill a ¾-inch hole in the head for the eye. Drill 1-inch holes for the handle (through the head and legs); also drill a 1-inch hole

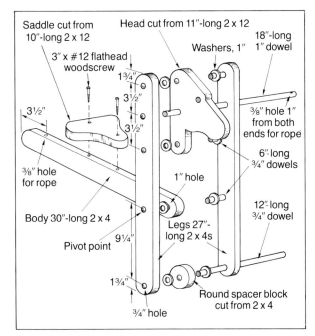

Drawing 1

through the body at the pivot point. Sand each part, rounding all edges.

From the ¾-inch dowel, cut one 12-inch-long piece for the footrest and three 6-inch-long pieces. Put them into the appropriate holes in one leg piece. Slide a washer over each dowel. Next, put on the head, body, and spacer; then add the last four washers. Finally, position the other leg.

Make sure that the body pivots freely; then lock the short dowels into position, using glue and finishing nails driven into the dowels through the front of each leg. (Drill pilot holes to prevent splitting.) Trim off excess dowel and sand smooth. Push the handle (the 1-inch dowel) through the holes drilled for it in the head and legs, and push the footrest (the ¾-inch dowel) through the legs and the spacer. Center the handle and the footrest and lock both into place with finishing nails.

Glue and screw the saddle into position, adjusting its position to the length of the child's legs. Drill ⅜-inch holes for rope in the handle and body. Seal the wood with several coats of a clear, nontoxic wood preservative.

Hang the swing with ⅜-inch rope through the holes drilled in dowel handles and body. (If you use synthetic rope, you can stop the ends from fraying by melting them with a match.) Hang the swing where there's lots of room—a vigorous swinger can make the horse move slightly from side to side, as well as back and forth. Depending on the lengths of the ropes, adjust the distance between the suspension points for a stable ride, but be sure they're no further apart than 24 inches.

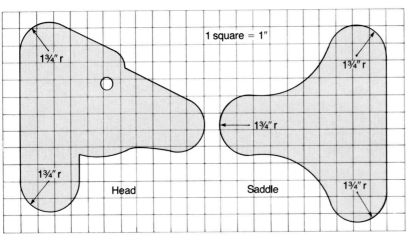

1 square = 1"

1¾" r

1¾" r

1¾" r

1¾" r

1¾" r

Head

Saddle

Drawing 2

ROLLING WOOD TOY

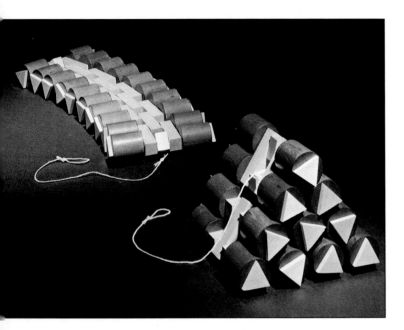

This little wood toy gets around with the greatest of ease—climbing stairs, rolling downhill, and trundling along behind its leader. Fold or stack it to make any shape you want. You can buy all the components at the wood molding department of a lumberyard.

Materials list

4' of 1¾" pine round
4' of 1 by 1 square pine molding
2' of 3/16" by 1⅜" pine lattice
6' of 3/8" hardwood dowel
Dark stain
Clear nontoxic wood sealer
Glue
String
1 eyescrew

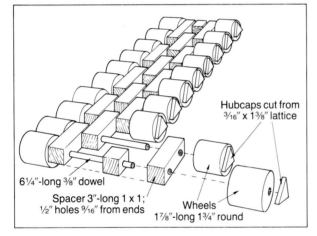

Hubcaps cut from 3/16" x 1⅜" lattice

6¼"-long 3/8" dowel

Spacer 3"-long 1 x 1; ½" holes 9/16" from ends

Wheels 1⅞"-long 1¾" round

Cut the pine round into twenty 1⅞"-inch-long wheels. Using a drill press or a hand-held drill with the wheels locked in a vise, drill 3/8-inch axle holes exactly in the center and exactly perpendicular to the wheels. (This isn't easy, so we've allowed enough round for four extra wheels if you make a mistake.) Sand the wheel ends, then stain wheels with a dark stain.

Cut the square molding into fifteen 3-inch pieces for the spacers. Mark points on each piece 9/16 inch in from the ends; then drill ½-inch holes. (These wooden spacers keep the wheels equidistant from each other and allow each pair to pivot freely.) For the ends of the toy, cut one spacer into two 1-inch pieces, trimmed so each hole is centered.

Make the eye-catching triangular hubcaps by cutting the lattice into equilateral triangles (60° at each corner) measuring about 1¼ inches per side. Finish the triangles, wheels, and spacers with a clear nontoxic sealer. Let dry completely.

For the axles, cut the 3/8-inch dowel into ten 6¾-inch lengths. Glue them flush into 10 of the wheels, then add wooden spacers as shown in the drawing at left. Glue the remaining 10 wheels in place (use glue sparingly; the wooden spacers must move freely on the axles). Center and glue a hubcap on the end of each wheel. To pull the toy, attach a long piece of string to an eyescrew in one of the middle end spacers.

BUILDING BLOCKS

Building blocks are perennial favorites of boys and girls. Just a few simple shapes can be combined to create castles, forts, houses, even little towns. To make a set of 69 blocks of assorted shapes and sizes, you need just three pieces of milled lumber (any species of wood free of large knots will do). Use two 4 by 4s, each 6 feet long, and one 8-foot-long 1 by 4.

From one of the 4 by 4s, cut 12 pieces, each 3½ inches long. Rip the remaining piece of this 4 by 4 into four lengths, 1¾ inches wide and 1¾ inches thick. From these lengths, cut 12 pieces 3½ inches long, four pieces 7 inches long, and four pieces 10½ inches long.

Rip the second 4 by 4 in half. From these two lengths cut 12 pieces 3½ inches long, eight pieces 7 inches long, and four pieces 10½ inches long. Make four triangles by cutting two of the 3½-inch pieces diagonally.

From the 1 by 4, cut six pieces 7 inches long and five pieces 10½ inches long.

Sand all the blocks, rounding all the corners. To finish the blocks, coat them with a sealer to enhance the natural color and grain, or spray paint them in bright rainbow colors. Be sure to use nontoxic materials.

BACK-YARD SANDBOX

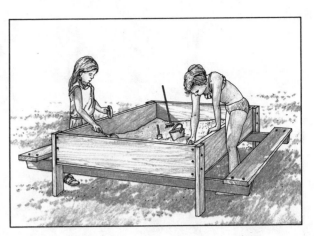

A sandbox is a wonderful place for children to play. The seating arrangement on this sturdy model provides plenty of room to share the fun with guests. As the seasons change, you can move the box to take advantage of sun or shade (several adults can lift it). You can also disassemble the box by removing the lag screws.

Cut lumber according to the dimensions in the drawing below. Assemble the 2 by 10 sides using three ⅜ by 3½-inch lag screws at each corner. Then screw the ¾-inch plywood to the bottom of the 2 by 10 frame, placing 2½-inch by #10 woodscrews at 8-inch intervals all around the edges.

Attach the 2 by 4 legs using ⅜ by 3-inch lag screws. Then attach the 2 by 4 seat supports and center support to the sandbox using ⅜ by 2½-inch lag screws screwed from the inside. Finally, attach the 2 by 8 seats to the seat supports using ⅜ by 3-inch lag screws.

If you wish, you can make a cover from ½-inch plywood; cut it the same size as the sandbox base. This comes in handy for keeping out rain and pets.

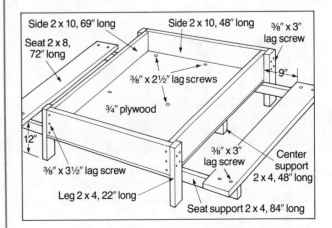

Side 2 x 10, 69" long
Side 2 x 10, 48" long
⅜" x 3" lag screw
Seat 2 x 8, 72" long
⅜" x 2½" lag screws
9"
¾" plywood
12"
⅜" x 3½" lag screw
⅜" x 3" lag screw
Center support 2 x 4, 48" long
Leg 2 x 4, 22" long
Seat support 2 x 4, 84" long

CHILD'S STORAGE CHEST

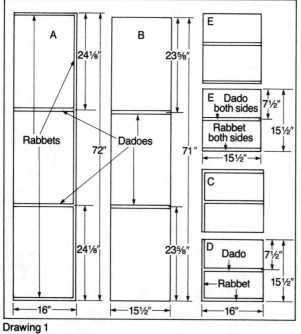

Drawing 1

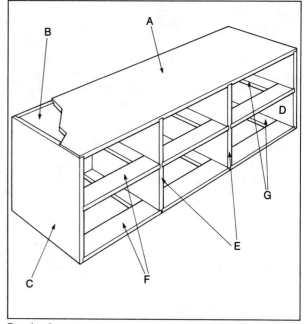

Drawing 2

This storage chest is just the right height for young owners. Its six roomy drawers offer plenty of storage space for clothes, toys, and assorted prized possessions. And if you add a cushion to fit across the top, the chest doubles as a comfortable bench.

You can use either fir or birch plywood for this project. Though birch plywood is more expensive than fir, you'll find it easier and faster to prepare for a paint finish.

Materials list

1 sheet of ¾″ fir A-B or shop birch plywood, 4′ by 8′
¼ sheet of ¾″ fir A-B or shop birch plywood, 2′ by 4′
½ sheet of ½″ fir A-B plywood, 4′ by 4′
¼ sheet of ¼″ fir A-B plywood or hardboard, 4′ by 4′
4d (1½″) finishing nails
4d (1½″) box nails
Glue

Following the cutting list below, cut pieces A through E. Cut the remaining pieces as you need them during construction.

A (Top panel): One @ ¾″ by 16″ by 72″
B (Back panel): One @ ¾″ by 15½″ by 71″
C and D (End panels): Two @ ¾″ by 16″ by 15½″
E (Center panels): Two @ ¾″ by 15½″ by 15½″
F (Bracing strips): Six @ ¾″ by 3″ by 23½″
G (Drawer runners): 12 @ ¾″ by 2″ by 12¼″
H (Drawer fronts): Six @ ¾″ by 6¾″ by 22⅞″
I (Drawer sides): 12 @ ½″ by 6¾″ by 14¾″
J (Drawer backs): Six @ ½″ by 6″ by 21⅞″
K (Drawer bottoms): Six @ ¼″ by 14¾″ by 22⅜″

As you work on this project, protect all plywood surfaces to prevent marring. Also, check frequently to make sure that all corners are square.

Cut ¾-inch-wide, ¼-inch-deep dadoes and rabbets in pieces A, B, C, D, and E, as shown in Drawing 1 (see page 88). Apply glue to the rabbet on the back edge of the top A and nail it to the back B with 1½-inch finishing nails. Glue and nail end panels C and D and center panels E to the top and back (see Drawing 2).

Working with the chest upside down, apply glue to the front 3 inches of the dadoes and rabbets in the center and end panels. Slip the bracing strips F in place; to ensure a tight fit, clamp them until the glue is dry, or toenail them. Apply glue to the remaining panel dadoes and rabbets and insert the drawer runners G. Use clamps to hold the runners in place until the glue is dry.

While the glue on the chest is drying, build the drawers (see page 91 for more information on building drawers). Cut out the drawer fronts H, sides I, backs J, and bottoms K according to the dimensions in the cutting list.

Make slots for drawer pulls by drilling two 1-inch-diameter holes on 2-inch centers in each drawer front. Cut out the remaining material to make an oval slot; rasp or sand smooth.

Cut ½-inch-wide, ¼-inch-deep dadoes and rabbets in the drawer fronts and sides (see Drawing 3). Then cut ¼-inch wide, ¼-inch-deep dadoes in the fronts and sides for the bottoms.

Glue and nail the drawer fronts, sides, and backs together, making sure the corners are square. As soon as the parts are assembled, slip the drawer bottoms in place to strengthen the drawers while the glue sets; don't use glue on the bottoms. When the glue is dry, drive 1½-inch box nails through the bottoms and into the backs to secure the drawer bottoms.

When all the glue is dry, sand and finish the chest and drawers as desired.

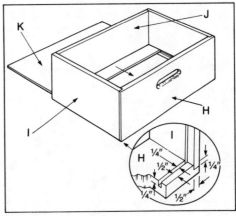

Drawing 3

TOY SHELVES IN HANGING BOXES

In a very short amount of time, children can amass an amazing number of toys. These hanging boxes provide an attractive home for dolls and other toys of all shapes and sizes.

Materials list

**For 3 shelving units, 19″ by 70″, 37″ by 58″,
and 25″ by 47″ (as illustrated):**
72′ of 1 by 12 pine: 3 @ 10′, 1 @ 12′, 5 @ 6′
14′ of 2 by 4 fir: 1 @ 6′, 1 @ 8′
6 flathead woodscrews, 1½″ by #8
12 lag screws, ¼″ by 3½″
Glue
6d (2″) finishing nails
Enamel paint and primer

Construction is simple—cut wood according to dimensions in Drawings 1 and 2. Then assemble all pieces with butt joints, using glue and finishing nails.

To hang the units, locate the studs in the wall. Then level and attach a predrilled length of 2 by 4 to the wall where each unit will hang. Cut the 2 by 4s to the inside width of each shelf unit; anchor them to the studs with ¼ by 3½-inch lag screws.

The shelves are hung from these 2 by 4s; a single 1½-inch woodscrew through the top secures them in place. A second length of 2 by 4 must be lag-screwed to the wall just above or below the next-to-lowest shelf of each unit to prevent any lateral motion. (A 1½-inch woodscrew through the shelf into the 2 by 4 provides additional rigidity.)

Finishing is fast. After a light sanding, paint the boards with a primer; then paint on one coat of enamel.

Design: Harley Licht.

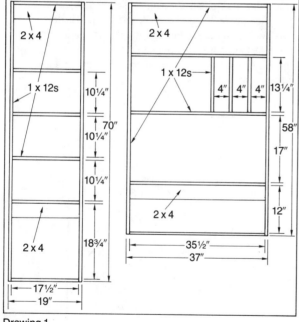

Drawing 1

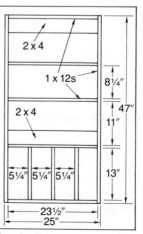

Drawing 2

ONE-PASSENGER BOAT

For young anglers and adventurers, this child-sized boat for one is a dream come true. Weighing about 40 pounds, it's easy for two children to carry. Though it's meant for carefree sport in calm water, safety always comes first. Any child using this boat should wear a life jacket and have confidence in the water. Let the boat cast off only in a well-supervised area.

Materials list

Lumber should be clear Douglas fir or equivalent.
12' of 1 by 8
8' of 1 by 4
4' of 1 by 3
3' of 1 by 1
4' of 1" hardwood dowel
½ sheet of ¾" A-B exterior fir plywood, 4' by 4'
10" by 12" piece of ¼" fir plywood
6d (2") galvanized box nails
14 galvanized flathead woodscrews, 1½" by #8
4 galvanized roundhead woodscrews, ¾" by #8
1 cartridge of silicone rubber sealant and a caulking gun
18" of ½" rope
1 quart spar varnish

From the 1 by 8, cut out two sides of the boat according to the dimensions in the drawing at right. Cut the plywood bottom pieces 2 inches longer than indicated, then bevel the ends, good side up, to the exact length needed. Using a caulking gun with silicone sealant, glue the bottom pieces together and to the sides; then nail at 3-inch intervals.

Next, cut the top and end pieces from the 1 by 4, beveling one long edge of each end piece to fit the plywood bottom pieces. Glue and nail the top and end pieces in place; secure the top pieces to each side with woodscrews (predrill and countersink holes). Bevel and cut the two 1 by 3 nailers; glue in place, using a generous bead of sealant, and nail down.

Use one of the corners cut from a side piece to make the rudder. Glue and nail the rudder and 1 by 1 keel along the center of the boat bottom. Also glue and nail the seat supports (cut from plywood scrap). Install the 1 by 8 seat, using three woodscrews in each end. Finally, drill two holes for the rope handle in the bow end piece.

To make the paddle, saw halfway through the 1-inch dowel 6 inches from each end, then slice the dowel in half lengthwise from the ends to the cuts. From the ¼-inch plywood, cut two blades (each about 5 by 12 inches); glue them to the flat surfaces at the ends of the

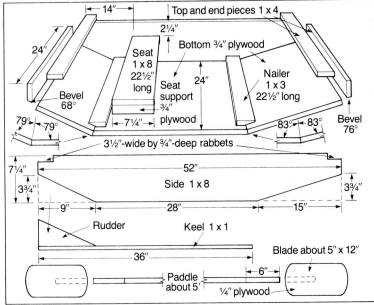

dowel and secure with ¾" screws. Or buy an adjustable metal and plastic kayak paddle (the adjustable length is desirable if children of different ages and sizes will use the boat).

Sand all boat and paddle surfaces; seal them with three coats of spar varnish, clear polyurethane exterior finish, or paint. Add the rope handle, paint on a name, and you're ready to launch.

Design: Lyon McCanless.

PLAYHOUSE

This playhouse is one project that's sure to see years of use by active, imaginative children. It will provide hours of fun as a house, a store, a secret hide-away, or just a special place for climbing, sliding, and crawling through.

Materials list

2 sheets of ½" exterior fir A-B plywood, 4' by 8'
54' of 2 by 2: 3 @ 8', 5 @ 6'
30' of 1 by 1: 5 @ 6'
2' of 1 by 3
4' of 1" hardwood dowel
8' of base molding
12' of plastic-coated chain (available at hobby or bicycle shops)
12" by 48" piece of plastic laminate
18" by 24" piece of matte black plastic laminate
5d (1¾") galvanized finishing nails
4 16d (3½") galvanized box nails
2 cabinet hinges
1 spring cupboard latch
Waterproof glue
Contact cement
Paint or sealer
24" by 60" piece of 3" foam rubber (optional)

Drawing 1

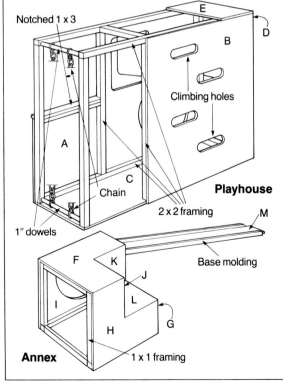

Drawing 2

Cut plywood pieces according to layouts in Drawing 1.

To build the playhouse, use 1¾-inch finishing nails unless otherwise noted. First, glue and nail 2 by 2 framing strips to side panels A and B (see Drawing 2). Glue and nail the bottom C to the framing strips at the lower edges of A and B. Glue and nail pieces D and E in place, with the side panels perpendicular to the bottom.

Predrill pilot holes into the framing strips for the nails that secure the dowels. Assemble the chain ladder and slide the ends onto the dowels. Then glue and nail the dowels in place, using 3½-inch box nails.

Notch the ends of the 1 by 3 window sill, then glue and nail it in place. The black plastic laminate serves as a chalkboard. Glue it to the outside of the door; trim the edges. Mount the door on cabinet hinges and install the latch.

Assemble the annex by first gluing and nailing the pieces F, G, H, and I together and reinforcing the corners with 1 by 1s. When the glue is dry, assemble pieces J, K, and L, reinforcing the corners with 1 by 1s.

Glue the plastic laminate to the slide M, using contact cement; trim the edges, if necessary. Glue and nail the base molding to the sides of the slide.

Round all corners of the units and sand well. Finish by sealing or painting the wood. Use the foam pad as a mattress for napping.

TABLE & PLAY-BLOCK CHAIRS

As if by magic, one sheet of plywood makes a whole set of versatile, low-cost furniture: four giant-size play blocks and a child-size table. Use bright-colored paints to decorate the blocks with eye-catching designs.

Materials list

For 4 blocks and 1 table:
1 sheet of ⅜″ fir plywood, 4′ by 8′
12″ of 2 by 4
13′ of ⅜″ by 1′ molding
3d (1¼″) finishing nails
6′ of 2″ PVC pipe: 4 @ 18″
16 roundhead woodscrews, 1″ by #6
Wood putty
Glue
Epoxy
White high-gloss enamel paint
Various bright colors of enamel

We used rabbet joints to minimize rough edges on the table and blocks. If you opt for speed rather than looks, cut all blocks about 1 foot square and use butt joints that you can later putty and paint.

To make the blocks with rabbet joints, cut eight pieces of plywood 11½ inches square (sides A in Drawing 1), eight pieces 11⅞ inches square (sides B), and eight pieces 11½ inches by 11⅞ inches (sides C). Make ⅜-inch-wide, ³⁄₁₆-inch-deep rabbet cuts around all edges of sides B; make similar cuts on tops and bottoms (11½-inch sides) of sides C. For extra support, nail as well as glue the sides together, using 1¼-inch finishing nails. Smooth exposed edges with wood putty; then sand, being careful to round all sharp edges.

Brush on two coats of white high-gloss enamel. Then use brightly colored enamel or acrylics to add play block or other designs.

To make the top of the table, use the 2 by 4-foot piece of ⅜-inch plywood that was left after you cut out the blocks; nail and glue the molding around the edges. From a scrap length of 2 by 4, cut four disks to the exact inside diameter of the pipe and epoxy them onto the underside of the tabletop at the corners, making sure the bond is strong (see Drawing 2).

To attach the legs, drill four holes in the top of each piece of pipe; push the legs onto the disks and screw 1-inch woodscrews through the holes to secure them. You can remove the legs for compact storage, or replace them with longer legs as the children grow.

Paint the table with high-gloss enamel to match the play blocks.

Design: Clifford & Cathy Monroe.

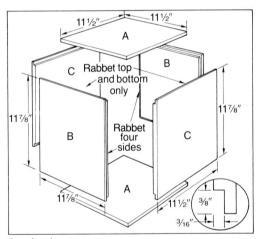

Drawing 1

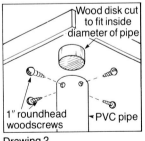

Drawing 2

SCOOTER PLANES

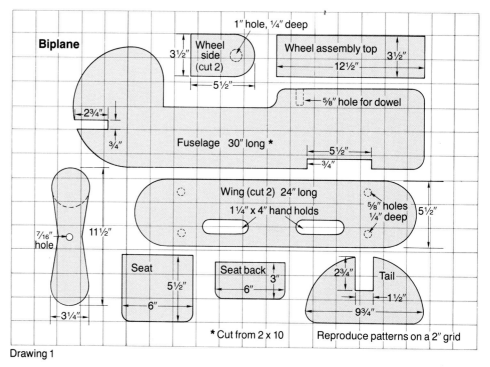

Biplane

1" hole, ¼" deep

Wheel side (cut 2)

3½"

5½"

Wheel assembly top

12½"

3½"

⅝" hole for dowel

2¾"

¾"

Fuselage   30" long *

5½"

¾"

Wing (cut 2) 24" long

1¼" x 4" hand holds

⅝" holes ¼" deep

5½"

7/16" hole

11½"

3¼"

Seat

5½"

6"

Seat back

6"

3"

2¾"

Tail

1½"

9¾"

* Cut from 2 x 10

Reproduce patterns on a 2" grid

Drawing 1

Fantasy flights and the wild blue yonder will fill all youngsters' imaginations as they take off on these scooter planes. The old-fashioned "tail-dragger" bi-plane and the sleek jet both roll on three wheels; they're easily managed by pilots up to six years old.

Materials list

For the biplane:
3′ of 2 by 10 *(for fuselage)*
6′ of 1 by 6 *(for wings, seat, back, and tail)*
3′ of 1 by 4 *(for wheel top and sides and propeller)*
13″ of 1″ hardwood dowel *(for axle)*
3′ of ⅝″ hardwood dowel *(for wing struts and joy stick)*
1 round wooden drawer pull *(for control knob)*
1 3″ caster and 2 5″ rubber-tired wheels
3 lag screws, ⅜″ by 4″, each with 2 washers
Glue

For the jet:
4′ of 2 by 10 *(for fuselage and control panel)*
10″ by 20″ piece of ¾″ plywood *(for wing)*
2′ of 1 by 4 *(for wheel top and sides)*
4′ of 1½″ closet pole *(for engines)*
6′ of 1 by 6 *(for seat)*
13″ of 1″ hardwood dowel *(for axle)*
10″ of ⅝″ hardwood dowel: 2 @ 5″ *(for joy sticks)*
2 round wooden drawer pulls *(for control knobs)*
1 3″ caster and 2 5″ rubber-tired wheels
2 lag screws, ⅜″ by 4″, each with 2 washers
Glue

Start either plane by cutting out all the pieces (see Drawing 1 or 2). Make the wheel assemblies separately from the bodies; the axles are counterbored ¼ inch into the inside faces of the vertical side pieces. First glue (do not nail) the axle into position; then glue and nail the wheel sides to the wheel assembly tops, using counter-sunk finishing nails. Before mounting the wheel assembly to the wings, drill ³⁄₁₆-inch pilot holes for lag screws, drilling through the sides and well into the dowel.

The biplane's wings should be assembled separately from the body. Cut five 7-inch pieces from the ⅝-inch dowel for the struts and joy stick. Counterbore four holes for the strut dowels ¼ inch into the inside faces of the wings. Glue and nail together before mounting the wings to the body.

The tail of the biplane should slide snugly into the notch cut into the fuselage. The control panel for the jet has a similar joint, but the notch isn't as deep.

When the bodies and wings are together, screw on the wheel assemblies, glue and nail on the seats, and glue in the joy sticks with knobs on top. Cut the closet pole for the jet engines, mitering one end of each piece, and glue and nail on.

Sand, seal, and paint the planes; then attach the wheels with ⅜ by 4-inch lag screws. (We left the bi-plane's propeller natural wood, then lag-screwed it to the front.) Paint your own insignia or buy large decals (available at some hobby shops).

When you're mounting the caster, you may find that the mounting plate is wider than the plane's body. In this case, add scrap blocks of wood to both sides of the plane to add width.

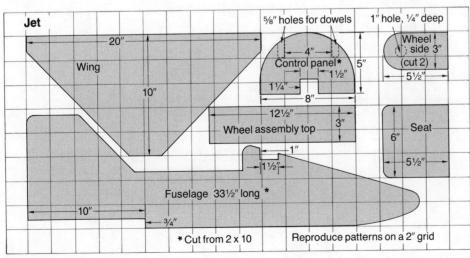

Drawing 2

MODULAR HOUSING

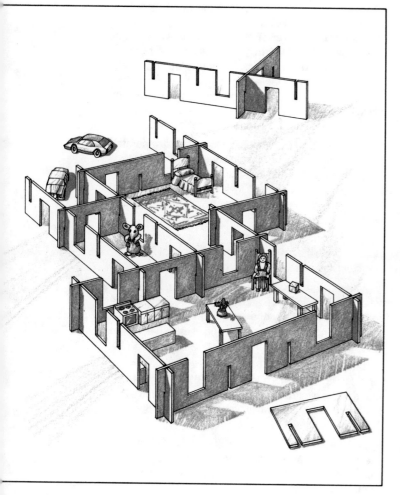

Dollhouse, schoolhouse, hospital, fort, farm, garage—your child's imagination is the only limit to the structures that can be made with these modular building boards. You'll find them economical to make: you can cut 28 units from a 4 by 8-foot sheet of ¼-inch tempered hardboard.

Following the cutting pattern in Drawing 1 will give you eight small units and 10 each of the medium and large ones. First, rip six strips, each 7⅞ inches wide. Then make shorter cuts, as shown, to divide the hardboard into A, B, and C lengths. (The small unlabeled pieces at the end of the sheet are scrap.)

Next, cut ⅜-inch-wide, 4-inch-deep slots 1 inch in from each end of all modules, and 8 inches in from the inside edge of these slots for modules B and C. (There should be 8 inches of wall space between the slots.) When you have cut all the ⅜-inch slots, cut 2½ by 6-inch door/window openings wherever you like. Alternate the direction of the door cuts on modules B and C, as shown in Drawing 2. If you like, cut a few modules without door/window openings to allow more wall space for furniture arrangement.

You can leave the hardboard as is or paint it. If you apply a coat of gloss white enamel, young architects can decorate the walls with crayons, then simply wipe them clean when they're ready for a new design.

To make multistory structures, cut floor dividers: square pieces with sides the same length as modules B or C. To make a roof, leave several modules without notches or door/window openings. These sections can be placed over the wall units to create a flat roof.

Design: William Crosby.

C		C		B		B	
C		C		B		B	
C		C		B		B	
C		C		B		B	
C		C		B		B	
A	A	A	A	A	A	A	A

Drawing 1

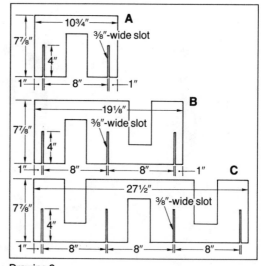

Drawing 2

PLAY CENTER

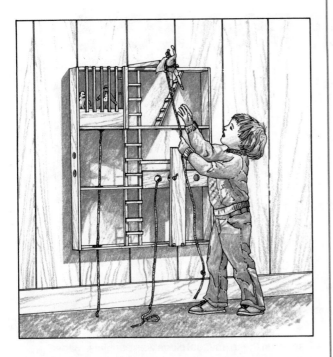

Kids can't resist the fascinating allure of this wall-mounted play center; it provides hours of imaginative play. You'll need pine 1 by 4s for the floors and walls and ⅛-inch-thick hardboard for the backing.

The drawing below shows a 30 by 36-inch play center, but you can adapt the dimensions to suit your needs. Keep ceiling measurements 10 to 15 inches high to allow headroom for your children's favorite action dolls. Before you assemble the play center (using glue, 3d [1¼-inch] finishing nails, and 1-inch brads), cut the doors, trapdoors, and portholes. Attach the unit to the wall studs with woodscrews.

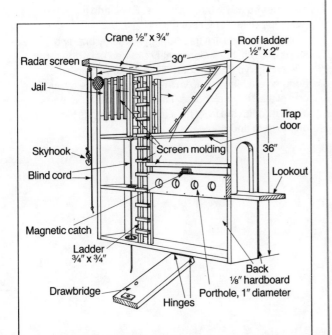

OUTDOOR SEAT SWING

Seven dowels, spaced ¼ inch apart, make the surprisingly comfortable seat of this swing. To make the swing, you'll need a 20-inch 2 by 3 (use redwood or a knot-free wood); four 36-inch-long ¾-inch hardwood dowels, each cut into two pieces, 17½ inches long; and enough ¼-inch rope to hang the swing.

Cut the 2 by 3 in half and round the ends. Next, clamp the two pieces together; center and drill ¾-inch holes for the dowels. Also drill holes for the rope. To keep the rope from pulling through the holes, put metal washers on the rope above the knots.

To hold the dowels securely, glue them in place, then drive 4d (1½-inch) finishing nails through predrilled holes in the bottom of each 2 by 3. Finish the swing with a clear, nontoxic wood sealer.

Design: Peter O. Whiteley.

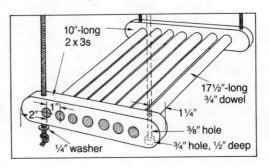

HOBBY & CRAFT PROJECTS

CENTIPEDE RACING CLOGS

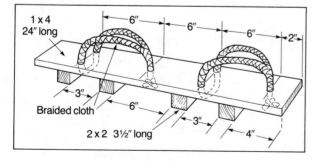

1 x 4
24" long

6"   6"   6"   2"

3"

Braided cloth

6"

3"

2 x 2 3½" long

4"

Racing on these unusual clogs was popular in Japan many years ago; later, the game found an enthusiastic following in Hawaii. Introduce the clogs at your next outdoor gathering to the delight of young and old alike.

The specially made *getas* (wooden clogs) can accommodate pairs, trios, or even quintets of racers, depending on the length you make them. We show two-racer clogs. The race itself is simple: the object is to be the first to march your geta-team over the finish line. The challenge is to keep your getas on your feet and your body off the ground.

Make your own multiple getas by gluing and nailing 3½-inch-long 2 by 2s to the bottoms of a pair of 1 by 4s; see drawing at lower left for the proper spacing. Use 4d (1½-inch) finishing nails for the job. Then drill ½-inch-diameter holes for the toe straps. Sand and finish the wood to prevent splinters.

The toe straps are traditionally made by braiding strips of cloth, but ⅜" or smaller braided or cotton rope will also serve the purpose. Thread each strap by bringing each end up from the geta underside through one of the two back holes. Then pass both strap ends down through the front hole and knot the ends together on the geta underside.

EASY-TO-MAKE WORKBENCH

Woodworking projects are easy to handle when you have a large, sturdy work surface and the "extra-hands" effect of table vises. You can put together this efficient piece of equipment in a single day.

Materials list

Maple countertop, 1½" by 25" by 60"
8' of 2 by 4 fir
12' of 4 by 4 fir: 2 @ 6'
4' of ⅜" threaded rod with 4 washers
     and 4 nuts
2 lag screws, ⅜" by 6", with washers
16 framing clips
64 roundhead woodscrews, 1¼" by #8
2 woodworker's vises
Bench dogs*
Glue

*Note: You may have to special-order bench
     dogs at your hardware or tool store, or
     you can make them from dowels.

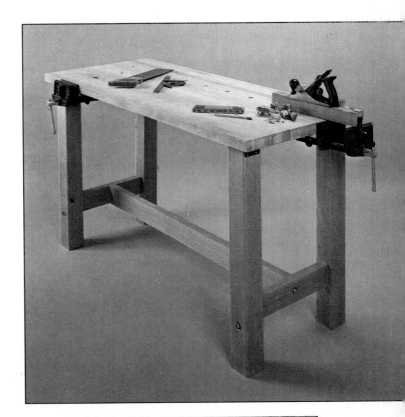

Start by cutting the lumber to the lengths shown in the drawing. Mark the center front of each leg 6½ inches from the bottom; counterbore for washers and nuts, then drill a ⅜-inch hole through each mark. Also drill a ⅜-inch hole through the center of each 15-inch 2 by 4 cross brace. Cut a 1½-inch-wide by ½-inch-deep dado in each one.

Next, cut a groove ¾ inch deep and ½ inch wide along the bottom of each cross brace; with a hacksaw, cut two 21¾-inch pieces of threaded rod. Assemble the legs and cross braces by running the rods in the grooves in the cross braces, then out through the holes in the legs. Secure with nuts and washers.

To complete the base, join each cross brace to the 51½-inch 2 by 4 rail with one countersunk ⅜-inch lag screw (see "Driving screws," page 93, for information on fastening into end grain). For added strength, glue all joints.

Position the countertop on the base and secure it to the legs with framing clips and woodscrews.

The real workhorses of the workbench are its end vise, front vise, and bench dogs (the rigid backstops for the vises that hold long or odd-shaped pieces of wood securely in place).

Mount the vises flush with the bench top, about 8 inches from the corners. Drill two rows of holes to fit your bench dogs, spacing them 6 inches apart and lining up each row with a vise. Round-shanked bench dogs can rotate to hold odd-shaped pieces tightly against the vise.

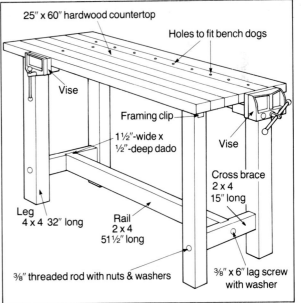

25" x 60" hardwood countertop

Holes to fit bench dogs

Vise

Framing clip

1½"-wide x
½"-deep dado

Vise

Cross brace
2 x 4
15" long

Leg
4 x 4 32" long

Rail
2 x 4
51½" long

⅜" threaded rod with nuts & washers

⅜" x 6" lag screw
with washer

SAWHORSES & PLANK

Tired of fussing with sawhorses that just don't suit your purposes? Here's an end to all your frustrations. These sawhorses have wide surfaces, making them suitable for many household needs, and they're extremely portable. So is the plank, yet it's strong enough to support the weight of several people.

Materials list

Lumber for sawhorses and plank should be redwood, fir, or pine.
For 2 sawhorses:
14' of 1 by 10: 1 @ 6', 1 @ 8'
4' of 1 by 4
16' of 1 by 2: 2 @ 8'
6d (2¼") galvanized box nails
Waterproof glue

For 1 plank, 8' long:
1 sheet of ¼" plywood, 4' by 8'
28' of 1 by 4: 2 @ 8', 1 @ 12'
6d (2¼") galvanized box nails
Waterproof glue

To make the sawhorses: Cut the lumber according to the dimensions in Drawing 1. Glue and nail the ends of the side braces to the legs with the legs set at an outward angle (see Drawing 2). When the glue is dry, set the leg assemblies on end with the side braces facing each other. Glue and nail an end and an end brace to two of the legs. Then set the assembly on its opposite end and attach remaining end and remaining end brace. Glue and nail the top in place.

To make the plank: Cut the plywood into two pieces, each 15¾ inches by 96 inches. Cut the 12-foot-long 1 by 4 into ten 14¼-inch-long cross braces. To make the frame, glue and nail the 96-inch-long 1 by 4 sides to the cross braces, spacing the cross braces evenly (see Drawing 3). Glue and nail the plywood sheets.

Design: Bob Meuser.

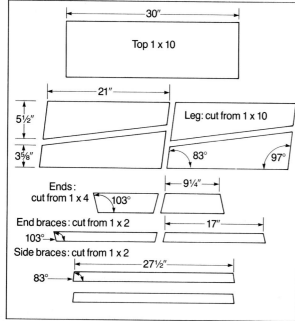

Drawing 1

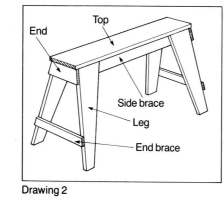

Drawing 2

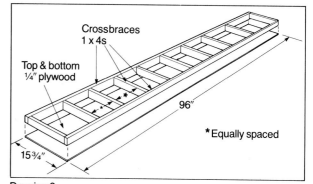

Drawing 3

DRAWING TABLE / DESK

Drawing table or desk? You probably don't have the space in your workroom for both. But with this one attractive piece of furniture, you can enjoy the convenience of both—and make a sound investment in dollars and space at the same time.

Materials list

1 sheet of ¾" birch plywood, 4' by 8'
5' of 1½" closet pole
6' of 2 by 4 clear fir
10' of 2 by 6 clear fir
49½" of ¼" quarter-round or other trim
Glue
12 flathead brass screws, 2½" by #12
1 piano hinge, 48" long, with screws
50" piece of ¼" by 5½" cork
Polyurethane

Precut the wood to the dimensions indicated in the drawing at right. Sand all surfaces smooth. Predrill holes for the brass screws, which fit through the end pieces into the 2 by 4 and 2 by 6 crosspieces. (See "Driving screws," pages 93–94, for information on securing screws in end grain.)

Assemble the end pieces and crosspieces using glue and screws. Glue and nail the quarter-round to the desk top; it will prevent pens and pencils from rolling off.

Finish all wood surfaces with three coats of polyurethane. When the finish is dry, use the piano hinge to attach the tabletop; insert the closet pole in one pair of holes and rest the tabletop on the pole.

To adjust the angle of the tabletop, just slide out the closet pole and replace it in another one of the three sets of holes. With the pole in the middle holes, the top is tilted at an angle of about 22½°, just right for sketching or drafting. For a sharper incline, place the pole in the highest holes. With the pole in the lowest holes, the tabletop lies flat.

Design: David Fitch.

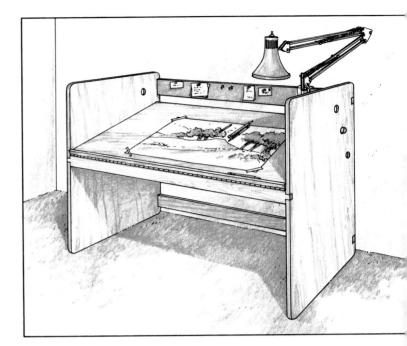

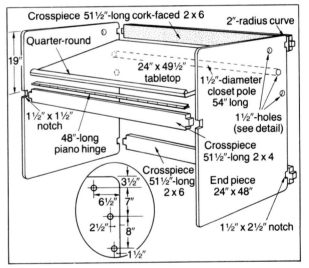

DISPLAY CASE

Collectors can proudly display their most treasured pieces in this wall-mounted case. You can adjust shelf heights to accommodate all kinds of small collectibles—from dolls to toy trains. The case's mirrored back helps show off each piece.

Removable glass doors protect your collection from dust. When you want to rearrange shelves, just slide the doors out.

Materials list

10' of 11½" vertical-grain fir stair tread
24" by 30" piece of ¾" A-D fir plywood
16" of ¼" hardwood dowel
12 flathead woodscrews, 2" by #8
20 flathead woodscrews, 1½" by #8
Glue
Wood putty
Clear finish
2 ¼" by 10⅝" by 28⅝" glass doors (ground edges)
4 ¼" by 4¾" by 21⅞" glass shelves (ground edges)
22¾" by 28¾" mirror
   (Do not order glass until you've checked measurements against the case's actual frame.)
2 flush wall-mounting brackets, with ¾" and 2" screws

Following the dimensions in the drawing on the facing page, rip and cut the stair tread to make the frame pieces. Cut rabbets along the square edge of each frame piece, as shown. Then miter both ends of each piece at a 45° angle.

On the top and bottom frame pieces, mark the placement of the 5/16-inch-wide, 3/8-inch-deep grooves for the glass doors. Cut grooves with a dado blade or a router. On the side frame pieces, mark and drill ¼-inch holes, ½ inch deep, to hold the shelf supports.

Align frame pieces; then predrill and counterbore holes for 2-inch woodscrews through the top and bottom into the ends of the side pieces. Glue and screw the frame, keeping the corners square, aligned, and flush. Check actual frame measurements against glass measurements. Make any necessary adjustments to the glass measurements; then order glass shelves and doors.

Cut the back to size from plywood. Sand and finish the inside of the frame. Install the mirror and screw the back into place with 1½-inch woodscrews. Fill all screw holes with wood putty, then sand and finish the outside of the frame. Cut sixteen 1-inch-long dowel pegs for shelf supports and insert them in the predrilled holes.

SPOOL ORGANIZER

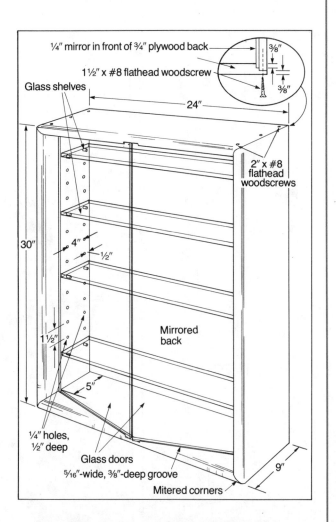

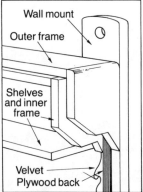

Position the display case on the wall and mark its corners on the wall. Check that the marks are level, then find the wall studs between the marks. Mark the stud location 6 inches below the marks for the top of the display case; transfer the measurements to the back of the case.

Screw wall-mounting brackets to the case back at the markings, using the ¾-inch screws. Then screw matching brackets to the wall studs at the markings, using the 2-inch screws. Hang the display case on the wall; add shelves, collectibles, and doors.

Design: Don Vandervort.

End sewing basket clutter and keep track of your thread inventory with this mini-shelf spool organizer. The 16⅝-inch by 20⅝-inch organizer has two frames. The inner frame and shelves hold the thread; the stepped-back outer frame masks the edge of the plywood back.

Materials list

24′ of ⁵⁄₁₆″ by 1¾″ pine lattice: 3 @ 8′
16″ by 20″ piece of ¼″ plywood
16″ by 20″ piece of black velvet
¾″ brads
Glue
Wood putty
Paint or clear finish

Start by cutting the lattice to size. For the inner frame, cut seven 19⅜-inch lengths (for top, shelves, and bottom) and two 16-inch lengths (for side pieces). For the outer frame, cut two 20-inch lengths (for top and bottom) and two 16⅝-inch lengths (for sides). Cut two 18½-inch lengths for the wall mounts.

Attach the velvet to the plywood back piece with a thin coat of glue. Let dry.

Assemble the inner frame so the bottom edge of the upper shelf is 3 inches from the top and the bottom edges of the other shelves are about 2½ inches apart. Sand, then finish, the inside surfaces of the inner frame and all of the shelves. Nail the fabric-covered plywood to the back of the inner frame.

Glue and nail the pieces of the outer frame in place, countersinking the brad heads. Fill the brad holes with wood putty; then sand. Before gluing and nailing the two mount pieces to the back, round one end of each and drill a ⅜-inch hole ¾ inch from the rounded end.

Finish the outer frame and wall mounts; then attach organizer to wall with pegs or screws.

FOLK TOYS

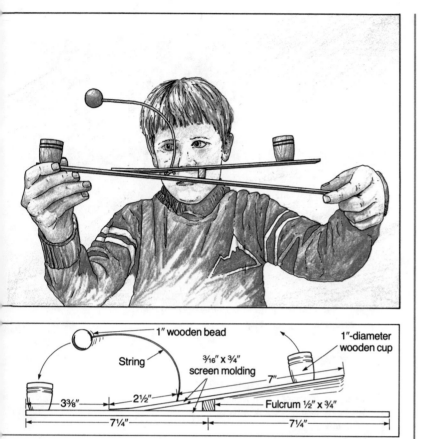

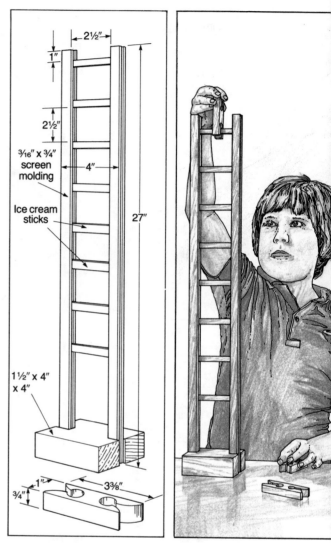

Folk toys and games, like folk tales, have existed for so long and been enjoyed in so many forms that their origins are a matter of speculation. Here are four toys your children can enjoy; with a little help, they can even make each one themselves.

FLIP BALL is a variation of an old game called *bilboquet,* which (in an ivory version) became the rage at the French court in the late 1500s. To play it, you try to flip a bead or ball from a cup mounted on a wooden spring strip to an identical cup mounted on a base piece.

Buy the 1-inch bead and the cups in a craft or hobby shop, choosing cups that fit the bead perfectly (if necessary, drill the cups yourself from blocks of wood). Cut the strips and fulcrum as shown in the drawing above. Glue the fulcrum and one cup to the base strip. Tie one end of a string through the bead and the other end through a hole drilled in the spring strip. Using the bead to guide placement, glue the second cup to the spring strip. Then glue the spring strip to the base.

PEG RACING is a competitive game that can be as addictive today as it was generations ago. You start grooved pegs on the top rung of a ladderlike structure and let them "race" to the bottom rung.

For the ladder sides, cut four 27-inch lengths of ³⁄₁₆ by ¾-inch screen molding. Lay two of the slats parallel, 2½ inches apart; then glue on rungs cut from ice cream sticks spaced 2½ inches apart. Glue the remaining two slats on top and let dry. Cut the base from a 1½-inch-thick block. Dado it to hold the ladder firmly; then glue the ladder in place.

Make pegs from wood scraps. The closer the holes, the more slowly and surely the peg moves; the farther apart the holes are, the faster the peg goes (but the more likely it is to fall off the ladder).

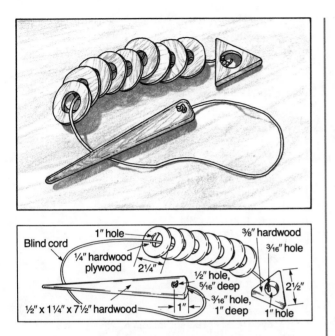

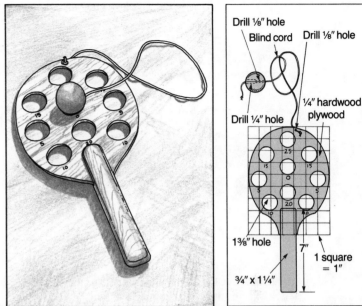

RING TOSS is played by swinging a group of rings on a string tied to one end of a wooden pin up in the air and trying to catch them on the pin's opposite end. After each try, rings that are caught are taken off the pin. If all the rings are caught at once, the player tries for the triangle. Each ring counts one point, the triangle 10 points.

To make this game, you'll need a 7½-inch-long piece of ½ by 1¼-inch hardwood, a 2½-inch-square piece of ⅜-inch hardwood, a 6 by 12-inch piece of ¼-inch hardwood plywood, and 28 inches of ³⁄₃₂-inch blind cord.

Taper the 7½-inch piece of hardwood down to a blunt point (see drawing above). Sand all the edges round and smooth. Drill a ³⁄₁₆-inch-diameter hole, 1 inch deep, in the bottom of the pin's wide end. Then drill a ½-inch-diameter flat-bottomed hole (use a ½-inch router bit) in one flat side of the pin, 1 inch up from the bottom; drill until the two holes meet (approximately ⁵⁄₁₆ inch). Push the blind cord into the small hole and out through the large hole; tie a knot in the end of the cord.

Draw ten 2¼-inch-diameter circles on the plywood. Drill a 1-inch hole through the center of each circle; then cut out the circles and sand the edges smooth.

Mark an equilateral triangle, 2½ inches long, on the ⅜-inch hardwood square. At the midpoint of one edge, drill a ³⁄₁₆-inch hole, ½ inch deep. Then drill a 1-inch-diameter hole through the center of the triangle, intersecting the first hole. Cut out the triangle; sand the edges.

Thread the rings onto the blind cord. Insert the free end of the cord through the hole in the edge of the triangle; then knot the cord inside the triangle.

BONUM BOARD is a game that tests your coordination. You swing a wooden ball tied to a paddle and try to catch the ball in one of the paddle holes. Each hole is assigned a number of points from 0 to 25. The object of the game is to score the highest number of points.

You'll need a 7 by 9-inch piece of ¼-inch hardwood plywood for the paddle; a 7-inch piece of ¾ by 1¼-inch hardwood for the handle; a 1½-inch-diameter wooden ball; and 25 inches of ³⁄₃₂-inch blind cord. You can make the bonum board with a ping-pong paddle (you won't be able to cut as many holes, though).

Drill nine 1⅜-inch-diameter holes in the paddle: seven around the edges and two in the middle (see drawing above). Drill a ⅛-inch hole through the paddle near the top edge, above and slightly to the right of the uppermost 1⅜-inch hole. Thread the blind cord through the ⅛-inch hole and tie a knot in the end.

Drill a ¼-inch hole two-thirds of the way through the wooden ball, and a ⅛-inch hole through the remaining third. Push the free end of the blind cord into the ⅛-inch opening of the hole and out the wider opening. Tie a knot in the end of the cord, then pull the knot back into the hole.

Cut a 1⅞-inch-deep by ¼-inch-wide slot in one end of the handle. Glue the paddle into the handle and clamp the pieces together.

When the glue is dry, paint numbers under each paddle hole, as shown in drawing above. If desired, finish the paddle with shellac or varnish.

SKIMBOARD

Youngsters love the thrill of jumping onto a skimboard and riding the shallow surf toward the beach.

This skimboard is simple to make, inexpensive, and small enough to take along anywhere. You can tailor the measurements to fit individual requirements, but most youngsters find that a board about 2 to 3 feet in diameter is the best size. The simple disk is cut from ¾-inch exterior A-B plywood. The bottom edge of the skimboard (see drawing below) is shaped with a rasp and sandpaper; fill any voids with wood putty. After shaping and finishing the board, paint it with several coats of marine paint in colors of your choice.

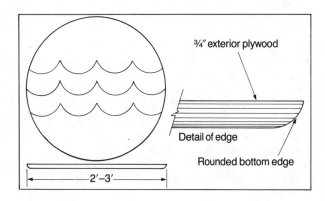

¾" exterior plywood

Detail of edge

Rounded bottom edge

2'–3'

SEWING CENTER

Here's a handsome piece of furniture that provides storage as well as work space for sewing. A counter flap swings up from the table to extend the tabletop work surface. In the cabinet, a pull-out shelf holds your sewing machine; a drawer above the shelf keeps sewing supplies within easy reach.

Materials list

1 sheet of ¾" birch plywood, 4' by 8'
¼ sheet of ¼" birch plywood, 2' by 4'
18' of ¾" by 1½" birch:3 @ 6'
1' of ¼" hardwood dowel
1' of ⅜" hardwood dowel
1½" (4d) finishing nails
1 box flathead woodscrews, 1½" by #8
12 flathead woodscrews, 2" by #8
3 2½" cabinet butt hinges, with
        ¾" woodscrews
2 pairs of 15" drawer glides
1 pair of pivot hinges
1 drawer pull
54" by 18" piece of plastic laminate
Glue
Contact cement
Wood putty
Clear finish

Cut plywood pieces according to cutting list below.

A (table & cabinet sides): Three @ ¾" by
        16½" by 27¼"
B (back crosspiece): One @ ¾" by 21"
        by 10"
C (lower shelf): One @ ¾" by 10½" by 16¼"
D (cabinet back): One @ ¼" by 11½" by 27¼"
E (tabletop): One @ ¾" by 16½" by 34½"
F (toe kick & drawer face): Two @ ¾" by
        12" by 3"
G (drawer sides): Two @ ¾" by 15" by 2¾"
H (drawer back): One @ ¼" by 9½" by 2¾"
I (drawer front): One @ ¾" by 8" by 2¾"
J (drawer bottom): One @ ¼" by 9½" by 15"
K (sliding shelf): One @ ¾" by 10¼" by 16"
L (shelf supports): Two @ ¾" by 2" by 16"
M (cabinet door): One @ ¾" by 12" by 20⅜"
N (tabletop extension): One @ ¾" by 16⅜"
        by 18"

Cut ½-inch-wide by ¼-inch-deep rabbets for the back D in the center and right cabinet sides A. Butt the back crosspiece B and the lower shelf C to center A; glue and screw in place with 1½-inch woodscrews. Glue and screw right A to C. Then glue and screw the cabinet back D to center A, right A, and C.

Lay the assembly flat, with crosspiece B and cabinet back D down. Glue and screw the tabletop E to the top edge of B and to center and right As, using six 2-inch woodscrews. Keeping all cabinet pieces square, glue and nail the toe kick F in place.

Cut the three tabletop extension slide support pieces from ¾-inch by 1½-inch birch; drill for screws and dowels. Glue and screw the slotted support to the underside of the tabletop E, using three 2-inch woodscrews.

Cut ¾-inch by 1-inch slots in the upper edge of left A (see Drawing 1); then glue and screw tabletop E to left A, using three 2-inch woodscrews; secure left A to back crosspiece B with glue and 1½-inch woodscrews. Invert the assembly, position tabletop extension N, and fasten it in place with three 2½-inch cabinet butt hinges secured by ¾-inch woodscrews. Insert the sliding supports and install ¼-inch dowel stops to retain them (see Drawing 1). Check that the extension is level when extended; if it's not, insert ¼-inch dowel spacers as indicated in Drawing 1.

Laminate tabletop E and extension N, using contact cement; sand or trim edges. Cut solid birch trim according to dimensions in Drawing 2; glue and screw in place, using 1½-inch woodscrews. Plug all screw holes with ⅜-inch dowel.

Build the drawer (see page 91) using pieces F, G, H, I, and J. (If your drawer glides *don't* require ½-inch clearance on each side of the drawer, adjust the drawer width accordingly.) Assemble the sewing machine pullout shelf, using the shelf K and shelf supports L. Mount the drawer and shelf on drawer glides.

Hang the door M on pivot hinges connected to the edge of the right cabinet side A.

Fill any nail holes on cabinet with wood putty; sand, then apply clear finish (mask off the laminate surface). Drill holes for the drawer pull and attach.

Design: Don Vandervort.

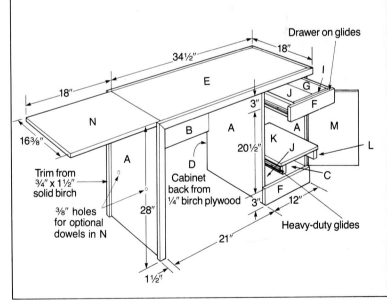

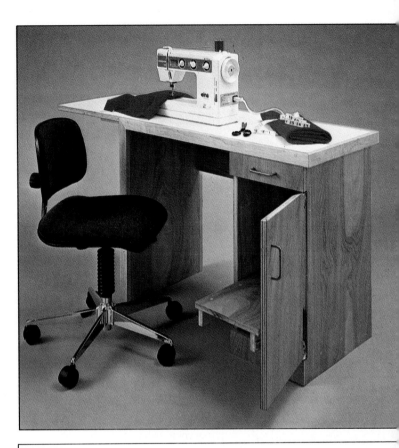

Drawing 2

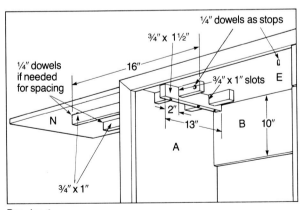

Drawing 1

GYMNASTIC EQUIPMENT

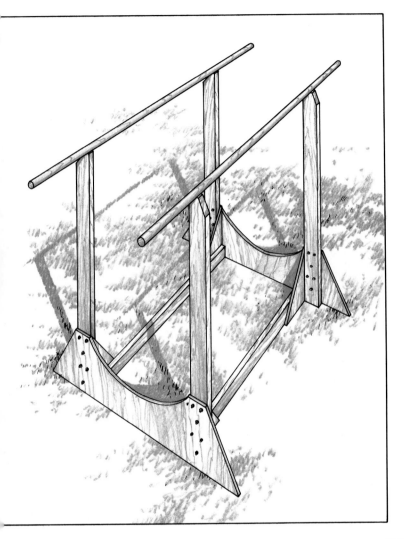

You don't have to be an Olympic hopeful to enjoy backyard gymnastics. These scaled-down pieces of equipment will encourage you to stretch, tone, and strengthen your muscles.

As you put the equipment together, keep safety in mind. Round all sharp edges and sand the wood until it's smooth and free of splinters. Set each piece up on a level surface (grass or ground, not concrete).

Follow the directions for each piece of equipment, using waterproof glue for all joints. Coat all surfaces with a nonslippery finish, such as a penetrating resin or satin-finish exterior polyurethane.

Shortened parallel bars

Use these for arm walking, arm dips, leg lifts, leg swings.

Materials list

12' of 1¾" banister rail: 2 @ 6'
30' of 2 by 4: 3 @ 10'
½ sheet of ¾" exterior plywood, 4' by 4'
6d (2") galvanized box nails
1' of ⅝" hardwood dowel
24 ¼" by 2½" carriage bolts (optional)
Waterproof glue

Saw tapered tops on the four 2 by 4 uprights; drill 1½-inch-deep holes for dowel plugs in the top of each (see drawing on facing page). Cut plywood gussets and supports as indicated; glue and nail the gussets to the 2 by 4 uprights and base pieces. If you want to be able to dismantle the bars for storage, attach the plywood supports to the uprights with carriage bolts. Otherwise, use nails and glue.

Drill a 1-inch-deep hole for a dowel plug 6¾ inches from one end of each banister rail, then insert a dowel plug. Carefully sight and drill holes at the other ends; glue dowels in place, attaching rails to uprights. Sand all edges; apply finish.

Low balance beam

Use this to practice splits, handstands, and walkovers, and to improve general balance.

Materials list

16′ of 2 by 4: 2 @ 8′
6′ of 2 by 6
2 2 by 6 joist hangers
Roundhead woodscrews, 1″ by #8, as
    required
Waterproof glue

Glue and clamp two 7-foot 2 by 4s together. (A single 4 by 4 will warp more easily.) Cut notches 3½ inches wide and 3 inches deep in both 8-inch 2 by 6s so the beam will fit snugly inside (see drawing below). Sand all edges smooth. Screw a metal joist hanger to the bottom of each notched piece. Position and screw on base 2 by 6s as indicated; apply finish.

Design: Diana Bunce.

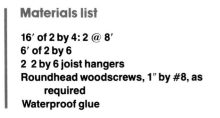

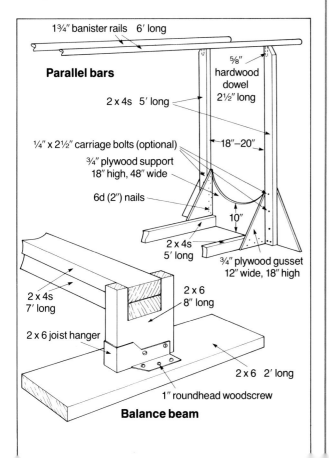

Parallel bars

1¾″ banister rails   6′ long
⅝″ hardwood dowel 2½″ long
2 x 4s 5′ long
18″–20″
¼″ x 2½″ carriage bolts (optional)
¾″ plywood support 18″ high, 48″ wide
6d (2″) nails
10″
2 x 4s 5′ long
¾″ plywood gusset 12″ wide, 18″ high
2 x 4s 7′ long
2 x 6 8″ long
2 x 6 joist hanger
2 x 6 2′ long
1″ roundhead woodscrew

Balance beam

SWEDISH RIBBSTOL

Use this piece of Swedish exercise equipment (pronounced *rib-stool*) for sit-ups, leg lifts, elevated push-ups, and ballet barre exercises. Children enjoy just scrambling up and down it.

From vertical-grain fir, cut two 95-inch 2 by 6s for the side frames and two 36-inch 1 by 3s for the back braces. For the rungs, cut fourteen 3-foot-long 1⅜-inch pine rounds.

Mark, then drill, 1⅜-inch holes for rungs in each frame side, 1⅝ inches from the front edge of each piece (see drawing below). Mark the lowest hole 4 inches from the bottom edge and the next 11 holes 5 inches apart; leave 12 inches to the thirteenth hole and 21 inches to the top hole. Cut ¾ by 2½-inch dadoes to hold the braces in the back edges of each frame piece, 1 foot from both ends.

Assemble the ribbstol on a flat surface. First, glue the rungs into the holes. Attach the braces with glue and 1½-inch by #12 flathead woodscrews. Fasten braces to wall studs with ⅜ by 3-inch lag screws and washers.

Design: Geraldine & Arthur Henry.

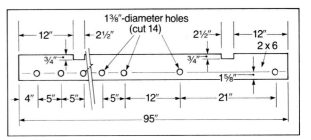

1⅜″-diameter holes (cut 14)
12″   2½″   2½″   12″
2 x 6
¾″   ¾″
1⅝″
4″ 5″ 5″ 5″ 12″ 21″
95″

YARD & GARDEN ACCESSORIES

GARDEN LIGHTS

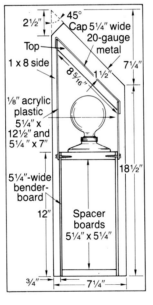

Light a footpath, illuminate your plants, or add a glow around your patio entertaining area with one or many garden lights. Each light is enclosed in its own weatherproof housing.

Materials list

For one garden light:
6' of 1 by 8 fir
2' of redwood benderboard, 5¼" wide
2 pieces of ⅛" smoked acrylic plastic:
   1 @ 5¼" by 12½", 1 @ 5¼" by 7"
5¼" by 11" piece of 20-gauge galvanized
   metal
Porcelain socket and round light bulb
2 roundhead woodscrews, ¾" by #8
4d (1½") finishing nails
Waterproof glue
Contact cement
Underground wire

The light housing offers an attractive variety of textures and colors. Hold the wood parts together with waterproof glue and 1½-inch finishing nails.

Inside, a single bulb is held in a porcelain socket wired to an underground cable. The drawing at left shows how the two acrylic sheets fit under the bent steel cap; each is held in place by a single ¾-inch woodscrew. Attach the metal cap to the top with contact cement.

Design: William P. Bruder.

OUTDOOR LANTERNS

Japanese-style lanterns add a romantic glow to an outdoor party with diffused light at entries, along paths, or on decks or patios. Each lantern holds up to four votive candles in glass cups; control the level of light by varying the number of candles. Though the lantern itself is lightweight and easily transportable, the base is stable, so there's little danger of tipping.

Materials list

For one lantern and shade:
7¼″ square of 1 by 8 pine
4′ of ⅜″ hardwood dowel
21′ of ¼″ by 1⅜″ pine lattice
1 yard of 22″ medium-weight nonwoven
        interfacing
Waterproof glue
Masking tape
Votive candles with glass containers

Cut the base from the 1 by 8 as shown in the drawing at right. Cut the lattice into eight 16½-inch strips for the side strips of the frame, sixteen 6⅛-inch strips for the top and bottom, and one 6½-inch and one 7½-inch strip for the handle.

For the double-layered bottom of the shade frame, position four 6⅛-inch lattice strips as in drawing. Spread these strips with glue; then stack four more strips on top, overlapping the corners. Repeat for the frame top.

When the glue is dry, stack the frame ends and tape them to each other. Cut each corner at a 45° angle, creating four 1½-inch flat spots. Sand.

Mark centers of two opposite sides and drill a ⅝-inch-diameter hole at each point. Position the stack over the base and mark centers of holes on base. Remove stack and drill a ⅜-inch-diameter hole halfway through the base piece at each point marked. Cut two 22-inch lengths from the dowel and glue them into the base holes, making sure they're perpendicular to the base.

Set one 16½-inch side strip on a flat surface and spread glue on the inner side of each end. Carefully glue one corner of each of the shade frame ends over strip (see drawing at right). Spread glue on the ends of a second 16½-inch strip and glue to opposite corners on the frame's end pieces; tape until the glue is dry. Glue on the two remaining 16½-inch strips. Let dry.

Brush glue on the outside of frame's side strips. Attach interfacing to the frame, starting at one side strip and aligning edges at top end; trim excess fabric from bottom end. Apply glue thickly on interfacing over the

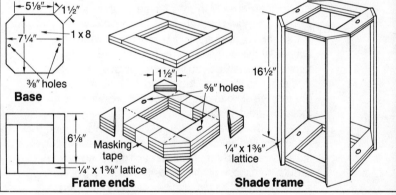

Base

Frame ends

Shade frame

side strips; glue the 16½-inch outer strips in place. Tape the strips to the base until the glue is dry.

Fit the frame over the dowels in the base. To make the handle, drill ⅜-inch holes in the 7½-inch lattice strip; glue it to the dowels. Center and glue the 6½-inch lattice strip on top.

Slide the shade frame up along the dowels to position and light candles.

DECORATIVE MAILBOX

RUGGED SAWBUCK

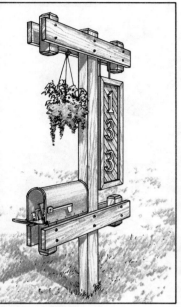

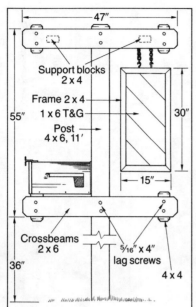

Most mailboxes are mere letter drops, but not this one: it also displays easy-to-read house numbers and a plant in a hanging basket.

Use redwood, cedar, cypress, or pressure-treated lumber for this outdoor fixture (see drawing above for the sizes of wood you'll need). The U.S. Postal Service requires that a mailbox be 36 to 48 inches above ground; the dimensions given for this project place the mailbox about 42 inches above ground.

Set the 11-foot-long 4 by 6 post 3 feet into concrete. Attach the two pairs of 2 by 6 crossbeams with 4-inch lag screws, being sure to offset each pair of screws to avoid hitting those on the opposite side. Also use lag screws to attach 7-inch-long beveled 4 by 4 blocks between the crossbeams at the outer ends.

Nail the bottom of the mailbox to the top of one of the 4 by 4 blocks between the lower crossbeams. Cut support blocks of 2 by 4 and nail them between the upper set of crossbeams. Hooks screwed into the bottoms of these blocks hold the chains for the hanging basket and the house sign.

Make the sign of 1 by 6 tongue-and-groove boards cut at 45° angles. Then frame the sign with 2 by 4s routed to fit; miter the corners. Purchase the large numbers at a hardware store.

Design: Dave Perce.

A sawbuck makes the task of cutting wood much more manageable. It securely holds any size log or branch while you saw it into firewood lengths.

To make this heavy-duty sawbuck, you'll need two 7-foot pieces of 4 by 4 rough redwood (or equivalent), one 8-foot length of 2 by 4 Douglas fir, 2 feet of ⅞-inch hardwood dowel, and 16d (3½-inch) galvanized nails.

First, cut the 2 by 4 into four 24-inch lengths for the cross braces. Then cut the 4 by 4s into 42-inch lengths.

Cross each pair of 4 by 4s about a foot down from the top, leaving a 2-foot spread at the base. Mark the intersections and notch them about 1½ inches deep. Make 1-inch-deep notches for the cross braces.

Join the 4 by 4s by drilling holes for 3½-inch-long dowels and pounding them in. Use 16d (3½-inch) nails to anchor the 2 by 4s.

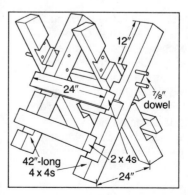

WHIRLIGIG

Add whimsy to your garden with a folk-inspired whirligig that moves about at the whim of the wind. As the propeller rotates, so does the wire attached to it. The wire, in turn, activates the figure on the stand.

Cut out all the pieces according to the dimensions in Drawings 1 and 2. Cut the propeller blades, horse pieces, and leg supports from ¼-inch hardboard. Glue the two pieces for the horse together with waterproof glue. Drill the holes in the horse and leg supports. Cut the propeller hub, the base, and the cap from clear pine or redwood (or other clear species).

Drill a ⅛-inch center hole in the propeller hub; also drill an offset hole for the ⅛-inch shaft wire about ¾ inch from the centered hole. In the hub edges, cut four equally spaced ¼-inch-wide, ¾-inch-deep grooves at 45° angles, as shown. Coat the ends of the blades with waterproof glue and insert them in the hub slots. Secure them with ¾-inch brass brads driven through the hub face.

Cut a ³⁄₁₆ by ³⁄₁₆-inch groove along the center of the top edge of the base to hold the propeller shaft wire. Also cut out the notch as shown.

Use an 18-inch length of ⅛-inch steel wire for the shaft. Bend one end into a "J" shape; when you slide the long leg through the center hole of the propeller hub, the short leg should enter the offset hole about ½ inch. Thread three ⅛-inch washers on the shaft and set the shaft and propeller assembly in the groove. Mark the wire for the offset position; then remove it and bend it into shape, making four 90° bends (see Drawing 1). Cut off the excess wire so the shaft fits in the groove.

Place the shaft and propeller assembly back into the groove, positioning the washers as shown. Apply grease in the groove to make sure the shaft rotates freely. Glue and nail the cap in place, using 1½-inch panel nails. Predrill if there's a danger of splitting. Secure the leg supports to the base using waterproof glue and ¾-inch brass brads. Attach the horse to the supports as shown, using a stove bolt, washers, and a locknut. Make sure that the horse pivots freely.

Loop one end of a 9-inch length of piano wire around the offset in the shaft and twist it as shown. Turn the offset in the shaft to the down position and position the horse's front hoofs about ½ inch above the cap; then slip the other end of the wire through the ⅛-inch hole in the horse's front leg and twist it around itself, making a loose loop. Test the action by turning the propeller; adjust piano wire, if necessary. Cut off the excess wire.

Support the finished whirligig from underneath and locate the center of balance. Mark it, then drill a 1-inch-deep hole for the ⅜-inch copper tubing. Glue the tubing in place.

Sand and finish as desired. Drive a 16d (3½-inch) finishing nail into the top of a post, and place a ¼-inch washer over it. Mount the whirligig on the nail.

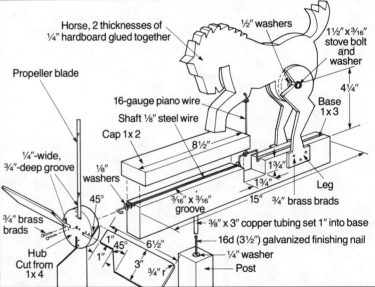

Drawing 1

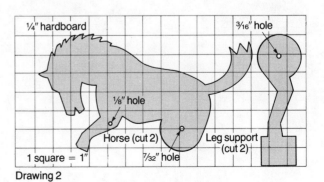

Drawing 2

HANGING BIRD FEEDER

This platform feeder offers a tranquil dining room for hungry birds and keeps mischievous cats and scavenging squirrels at bay. The feeder hangs from a slippery 7-foot-tall pipe system braced by a 4 by 4 post sunk in concrete.

Materials list

Lumber should be redwood or equivalent, such as cedar or cypress.
10′ of 1 by 1: 1 @ 4′, 1 @ 6′
14′ of ½ by 4: 1 @ 8′, 1 @ 6′
6′ of ½ by ½
10′ of 1 by 4
4′ of 4 by 4
10′ of 1″ galvanized pipe: 1 @ 7′, 1 @ 3′
Galvanized pipe sweep elbow, 1″
1 1″ coupling
2 eyebolts, ¼″ by 2″, with nuts and washers
6 S-hooks
Brass chain, ½″ (4 times the distance from pipe to platform)
4 eyescrews
2 1″ pipe clamps
¾″ brads
4d (1½″) galvanized finishing nails

First build the inner frame of 1 by 1s according to the drawing at left. Then cover it with seven ½ by 4 slats to make the feeding platform (rip one of the slats, if necessary, to make an accurate fit). Add eyescrews to corners of slat flooring. Nail the ½ by ½ strips for the food trap to the platform top. Cut the miter 1 by 4s for the outer frame; nail in place.

Dig a hole for the 4 by 4 post and set it 2 feet into concrete. Assemble the pipe and attach it to the post with pipe clamps. Suspend the platform from eyebolts with S-hooks and brass chain.

Camouflage the pipe stand by planting honeysuckle at the base and training it up the pipe. The honeysuckle's stems are too flimsy to support a cat or squirrel, and its flowers attract hummingbirds.

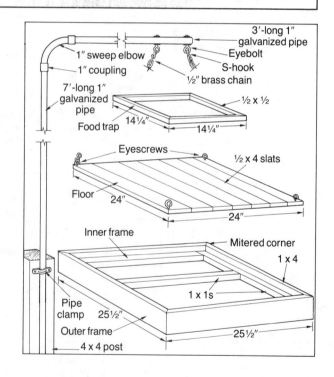

CUSTOM-MADE BIRDHOUSE

Build a home for a family of birds, and you'll soon be rewarded with hours of bird-watching pleasure.

Before you begin building, become acquainted with the types of birds likely to nest in your area. Each species requires different accommodations. For example, a shoe-box-size structure with a 2-inch hole won't attract the wrens that fly by. They simply won't use it: it's too large to be cozy, and the 2-inch opening will allow larger birds to enter and threaten the occupants.

The chart below lists some familiar garden birds that will nest in manmade houses, and gives specifications for their needs in house size, diameter of opening, and height of opening from the house's floor. It also gives the height above ground that the house should be mounted. You can use any ½ or ¾-inch lumber to build the house.

Species	Floor of Cavity	Depth of Cavity	Entrance above Floor	Diameter of Entrance	Height above Ground
	Inches	Inches	Inches	Inches	Feet
House finch	5x5	8	6	1½	5–10
Robin	6x8	8	*	*	6–15
Black-capped chickadee	4x4	8–10	6–8	1⅛	6–15
Tufted titmouse	4x4	8–10	6–8	1¼	6–15
Nuthatch	4x4	8–10	6–8	1¼	12–20
House wren	4x4	6–8	1–6	1–1¼	6–10
Bewick's wren	4x4	6–8	1–6	1–1¼	6–10
Carolina wren	4x4	6–8	1–6	1½	6–10
Violet-green swallow	5x5	6	1–5	1½	10–15
Tree swallow	5x5	6	1–5	1½	10–15
Barn swallow	6x6	6	*	*	8–12
Purple martin	6x6	6	1	2½	15–20
Starling	6x6	16–18	14–16	2	10–25
Black and eastern phoebe	6x6	6	*	*	8–12
Common flicker	7x7	16–18	14–16	2½	6–20
Red-headed woodpecker	6x6	12–15	9–12	2	12–20
Downy woodpecker	4x4	9–12	6–8	1¼	6–20
Hairy woodpecker	6x6	12–15	9–12	1½	12–20
Screech owl	8x8	12–15	9–12	3	10–30

*One or more sides open.

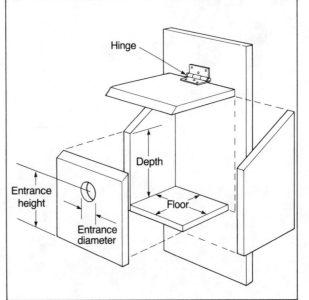

HANGING PLANT SHELF

Make an impressive eye-level display by grouping several small plants on this spacious hanging shelf. The open design allows air to circulate around the plants and makes the shelf surprisingly lightweight.

Materials list

For one 2′ by 4′ shelf:
8′ of 2 by 6 clear redwood or cedar
30′ of 2 by 2 clear redwood or cedar: 3 @ 8′,
**   1 @ 6′**
57″ of ¼″ metal rod: 3 @ 19″
Scraps of ¼″ hardwood dowel
8 ceiling hooks
Chain (4 times the distance from ceiling to
**   shelf height)**
Waterproof glue
Polyurethane penetrating oil sealer
**   (optional)**

Cut 4-foot lengths from the 2 by 6 (for the sides) and the three 8-foot 2 by 2s (for the bottom). From the 6-foot 2 by 2, cut five 2-inch pieces (for blocking in the middle to prevent warping) and ten 5½-inch pieces (for spacers at the ends).

The 19-inch rods reinforce the shelf. Carefully drill holes through the ends and middle of the wood to receive the rods, making sure that the holes line up. Drill through both 2 by 6s simultaneously; then use one of them as a pattern. Lay it on top of each 2 by 2 and mark through the already-drilled hole; drill holes through the 2 by 2s.

To assemble the planter, push a rod through the end of one 2 by 6, then a 4-foot 2 by 2, then a 5½-inch 2 by 2, and so on as shown in drawing at left, using glue where pieces join. Line up pieces carefully. Tap the end of the rod until it is slightly recessed.

Following the same procedure, push rods through the middle of the planter (using the 2-inch 2 by 2s as spacers) and the other end. Use large clamps to hold the shelf together until the glue is dry. Fill the rod holes with pieces of dowel and sand smooth. If desired, finish with a polyurethane penetrating oil sealer.

Predrill holes for ceiling hooks. Screw in hooks and hang the shelf on chains from hooks in the ceiling rafters or a roof overhang.

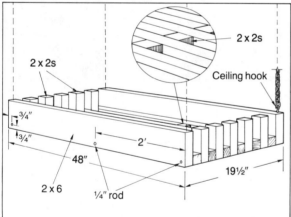

GARDEN PLANTER

The curved trim on this six-foot-long garden planter provides a decorative edge to a functional project. Use the planter as a display box for flowers or as a container garden for vegetables.

Materials list

24' of 1 by 12 rough redwood: 4 @ 6'
40' of 1 by 3 rough redwood: 4 @ 6', 2 @ 8'
8d (2½") galvanized box nails
4d (1½") galvanized finishing nails

Cut the 6-foot pieces of 1 by 3 into 5-foot lengths. From the remaining scraps, cut four 4-inch lengths. From the two 8-foot pieces of 1 by 3, cut two 6-foot 4-inch pieces and two 1-foot pieces.

Cut one of the 1 by 12s into eight 6-inch lengths (for C-shaped trim) and two 11-inch lengths (for box ends).

With a helper holding the pieces in place, nail together the remaining three 6-foot lengths of 1 by 12 (for the box sides and bottom) and the two 11-inch lengths (for the box ends). Drive 2½-inch nails every 8 inches along the bottom and every 3 inches at ends, alternating angles for more strength. Drill pilot holes to avoid splitting the wood.

On each of the eight 6-inch 1 by 12s, draw a semicircle with a diameter of about 6 inches. Cut out the semicircles with a saber saw and nail a C-shaped piece in place at each corner of the box, using 1½-inch nails. Drill pilot holes to avoid splitting the wood.

The C-shaped trim on the box ends will be 4 inches apart (see drawing at right). Fit in and nail down two of the 4-inch lengths of 1 by 3 at each end.

Complete the trim pattern by nailing the four 5-foot 1 by 3s in place along the box sides. Then nail the remaining 1 by 3s around the top edge to make a rim.

To finish, drill several ½-inch holes in the bottom for drainage.

Design: Max Hartstein & Jerry Barnes.

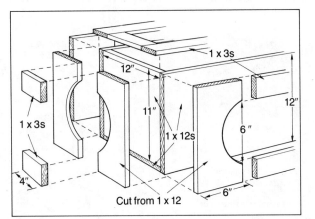

GARDEN PLANTER/BENCH

Whether you prefer to sit in the shade of small planter trees or relax amid the fragrance of your favorite flowering plants, this garden planter/bench offers a perfect outdoor retreat.

Materials list

24' of 2 by 4 clear redwood or cedar: 4 @ 6'
16' of 2 by 6 clear redwood or cedar: 2 @ 8'
50' of 2 by 8 clear redwood or cedar: 3 @ 14';
    1 @ 8'
¼ sheet of ¾" exterior fir plywood, 2' by 4'
12 ¼" by 2' threaded rods, each with
    2 washers and 2 nuts
48 lag screws, ¼" by 3"
6 lag screws, ⅜" by 2¾", with washers
12d (3¼") galvanized finishing nails
9d (2¾") galvanized common nails
Wood putty
Water-repellent wood preservative

Cut all pieces, following the cutting list below. Miter one end of each piece C at a 45° angle as shown in Drawing 1.

A (container base sides): Four 2 x 4s @ 17"
B (container base fronts & backs): Four
    2 by 4s @ 18"
C (container supports): Eight 2 by 4s @ 18"
D (container fronts & backs): Twelve 2 by
    8s @ 21"
E (container sides): Twelve 2 by 8s @ 20"
F (bench slats): Three 2 by 6s @ 48"
G (bench faces): Two 2 by 8s @ 48"
H (bench supports): Two 2 by 6s @ 17"
I (container bottoms): Two pieces of ¾"
    plywood @ 17" by 21"

To make each container base, butt two pieces B between two pieces A and nail in place with 3¼-inch finishing nails (see Drawing 1). Nail a plywood bottom I to the base, using 2¾-inch nails. Then drill five ¾-inch drain holes through the bottom piece I.

Mark each end of all side pieces E with the locations of the ¼-inch rods and ¼-inch lag screws (see Drawing 2). Counterbore ¾-inch-wide, ⁵⁄₁₆-inch-deep holes at these markings for the washers, nuts, and bolt heads. Continue drilling ¼-inch holes for the bolts and rods.

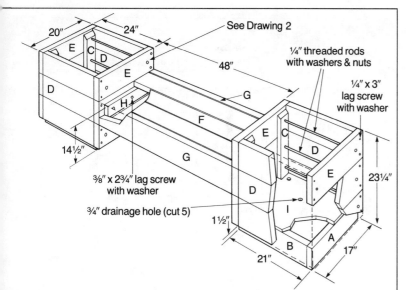

See Drawing 2

¼" threaded rods with washers & nuts

¼" x 3" lag screw with washer

⅜" x 2¾" lag screw with washer

¾" drainage hole (cut 5)

Drawing 1

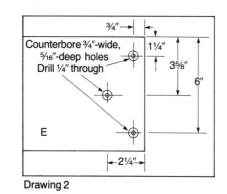

Counterbore ¾"-wide, ⁵⁄₁₆"-deep holes Drill ¼" through

Drawing 2

Lay four D and four E pieces flat. Using a combination square, measure 2 inches from the lower edge and mark a line along the length of each board at that measurement. To build each container, align the top edge of the base with the marked lines on two D and two E pieces, arranging the corners as shown in Drawing 1. Nail through the base into the container pieces, using 2¾-inch nails. Nail a support C, with mitered edge up, into each container corner, using 2¾-inch nails.

To finish each container, clamp four pieces E to the container supports C. Use the ¼-inch holes in all the pieces E as guides to drill through the supports. Position four pieces D between the sides E. Clamp them in place by inserting the rods, adding washers, and tightening the nuts. Then secure each piece D by inserting ¼-inch lag screws through the remaining holes in the sides E. Nail the supports C to the upper four sides E, using 2¾-inch nails.

Drill three ⅜-inch holes in each bench support H and bolt it to the containers with ⅜-inch lag screws and washers as shown in Drawing 1. Place the containers in their intended positions before attaching the bench.

Set the bench slats F on the supports H, spacing each slat evenly; nail in place with 3¼-inch finishing nails. Place the bench faces G against the front and back slat edges, keeping the top edges flush; nail in place with 3¼-inch nails.

Set all visible nail heads and fill the holes with wood putty. Sand all exposed surfaces, fill the planters, then sit back and enjoy your garden.

Design: Don Vandervort.

MINI-GARDEN PLANTER

This handsome planter showcases a garden of little perennials or provides a beautiful home for a prized bonsai tree.

Cut wood to the dimensions shown in the drawing below; then rabbet the lower edges of the 2 by 6 redwood pieces to receive the plywood bottom. Miter the corners and glue the four sides together with waterproof glue, holding them with clamps. (See page 88 for cutting rabbets and miters.) Let the glue dry overnight.

Shape the inner sides with a disk sander, applying unequal pressure to achieve undulating contours. Use a coarse, 20-grit, open-coat, silicon-carbide sanding disk; finish with an 80-grit disk.

Glue and nail the plywood bottom in place using 3d (1¼-inch) galvanized box nails. With a disk sander, round all the edges and shape the outer sides, tapering them to about a ⅞-inch thickness at the top. Nail two 1-foot 1 by 2 redwood strips across the bottom for cleats. Bore five ½-inch holes for drainage. Finish with a bit of hand sanding.

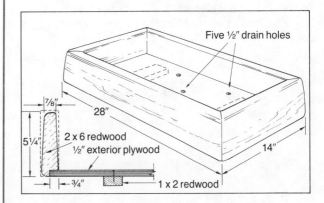

Five ½" drain holes

⅞"

28"

5¼"

2 x 6 redwood
½" exterior plywood

14"

¾"

1 x 2 redwood

PLANT POT SLEEVES/FIREWOOD BOX

Would you ever have thought that simple stacking and gluing could yield such spectacular results? That's all it takes to make these plant pot sleeves or an indoor firewood box.

For the sleeves (see Drawing 1), use fir or redwood 2 by 2s; the amount depends on the size of the desired sleeve. To build the firewood box (see Drawing 2), you'll need 33 feet of redwood 2 by 2s, 27 feet of fir 2 by 2s, and 5 feet of redwood 1 by 12. You'll need waterproof glue and, for the box, 8d (2½-inch) galvanized finishing nails.

To make plant pot sleeves: Stack and glue 8-inch-long 2 by 2s four tiers tall to cover a 6-inch-diameter pot, seven tiers tall to cover a 1-gallon can. Stack and glue 13-inch 2 by 2s nine tiers tall to cover a 5-gallon can. Coat the finished project with a clear wood preservative.

To make the firewood box: Cut the redwood 2 by 2s into 19 and 30-inch strips; cut the fir pieces into 16 and 27-inch strips. Stack the strips, alternating fir and redwood (use two 27-inch fir strips and two 19-inch redwood strips for the first layer). As you stack the strips, glue them at touching faces and nail them at the corners (predrill the holes). Form the handles by leaving out the sixth 2 by 2 from the bottom on the ends. Make the box bottom from a pair of 30-inch 1 by 12s ripped to 9½ inches wide. Nail and glue 1½-inch-long 2 by 2s to the corners.

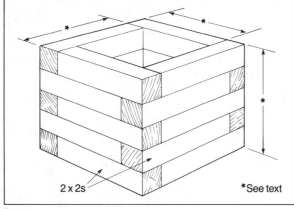

Drawing 1

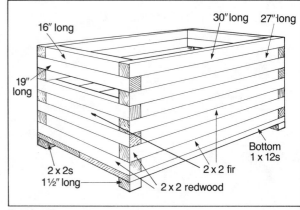

Drawing 2

TOOLS & TECHNIQUES

In this chapter, you'll find information on the types of tools suited to the woodworking projects in the book, and a discussion of each tool's functions. We also offer valuable information on buying wood and on many woodworking techniques, from measuring and marking to sanding, sealing, and finishing. Whether you're a novice or an experienced woodworker, you'll find tips in these pages to make your project more successful.

Unless otherwise specified, our projects can be made with hand or power tools. Whichever kind you prefer, buy them with quality—not price—as your first consideration. Top-quality tools are a good investment.

Buying wood

Before you make a trip to the nearest lumberyard, you'll need to know a few things. First, study the instructions for the project you plan to make, and write down a full list of the materials you'll need. Also determine which species of wood is best for your needs. You may want to shop around for the best price on lumber.

Dimension lumber

Dimension lumber includes hardwood and softwood boards sold according to specific widths and thicknesses. If you can't find lumber in the dimensions you need, you can have it specially cut. Make sure the wood you buy is suitable for your project in species and quality; it's also important to know how the wood was seasoned.

Types of lumber. Lumber is divided into hardwoods and softwoods. These terms refer to the origin of the wood: hardwoods come from deciduous trees, softwoods from conifers. Hardwoods are usually, but not always, harder than softwoods.

Hardwoods (mahogany, birch, cherry, and oak, for example) usually cost more than softwoods—but they also make more precise joints, hold fasteners better, and are more resistant to wear. If you have good woodworking skills and desire subtle grains or colors in your finished projects, use fine hardwoods.

Softwoods, such as pine, fir, redwood, cedar, and spruce, are much less expensive and more readily available than hardwoods. They're also easier to tool, making them a good choice for beginning woodworkers.

Seasoning. Seasoned lumber is either kiln-dried or air-dried. These two processes differ in the extent to which they reduce moisture content: the moisture content of kiln-dried wood is less than 8 percent, while that of air-dried wood ranges from 12 to 19 percent.

The best (and most expensive) grades of wood are usually kiln-dried. Kiln-dried lumber is primarily used indoors, but it also makes high-quality outdoor furniture when given a protective finish.

Most general construction work is done with air-dried wood. You can also use it for planter boxes and gym equipment. This lumber dries further as it ages and may shrink or contort; thus, it should be avoided for woodworking projects that require especially accurate measurements.

Quality. The amount of money you spend on lumber will be directly affected by the grade as well as the species of wood you choose. Whatever grade you buy select straight, flat wood; stay away from bowed, twisted, split, or warped pieces.

If you want the best softwoods, look for Clear, Clear All-Heart, Supreme Finish, Supreme, or B and better—the particular term depends on the species.

Softwoods designated Select Heart, Select, Prime Finish, C-Select, or Choice have slight defects.

The best grades of hardwoods are Firsts, Seconds, and a mix of the two called FAS. Next come Selects, which permit defects on the back, and Common 1 and 2. Lumber of lower grades than these is generally unusable if appearance is important.

Lumber sizes. Softwoods are sold in 2-foot increments, with lengths ranging from 6 to 20 feet. The measured thickness and width of a particular board depend in part upon whether it's rough or finished. Most of the projects in this book specify finished lumber; rough lumber has very coarse splintery surfaces.

The nominal dimensions of rough lumber are pretty close to what you get. In other words, a 2 by 4 is about 2 inches thick and 4 inches wide. But when that

Standard dimensions of finished lumber

SIZE TO ORDER	SURFACED (Actual Size)
1 x 2	¾" x 1½"
1 x 3	¾" x 2½"
1 x 4	¾" x 3½"
1 x 6	¾" x 5½"
1 x 8	¾" x 7¼"
1 x 10	¾" x 9¼"
1 x 12	¾" x 11¼"
2 x 3	1½" x 2½"
2 x 4	1½" x 3½"
2 x 6	1½" x 5½"
2 x 8	1½" x 7¼"
2 x 10	1½" x 9¼"
2 x 12	1½" x 11¼"

Thickness of 3" lumber is 2½"; thickness of 4" lumber is 3½".

lumber is dried and surfaced, as is done with all finished lumber, it ends up considerably short of the 2-inch and 4-inch dimensions. Nominal and actual sizes are shown in the chart at left below.

Hardwood lumber is often sold in odd lengths and sizes by the lineal foot, board foot, or even by the pound. When you need hardwood for a particular project, specify the size and footage you need and ask the salesperson to sell you the lumber in stock that will fill your requirements with the least waste. If possible, hand-pick your lumber.

Plywood

Plywood has several advantages over lumber: exceptional strength, high resistance to warping, availability in large sheets, and, in most cases, lower cost.

Like lumber, plywood falls into two categories: softwood and hardwood. The difference lies in the species of wood used for the outer faces of a panel.

Softwood plywood. This category includes Douglas fir, redwood, and cedar. The latter two are usually sold as house siding, but you can also use them for furniture projects.

Each face of softwood plywood is graded separately. Common grades run from A through D. Faces marked A have neatly made repairs and consistent color; D faces have large, unfilled knotholes and splits. B and C grades lie in between.

In general, A faces are suitable for natural finishes, B faces for stains, and repaired C faces (called C-Plugged) for painting. If a flawless appearance is important, look for N grade.

Plywood comes in several face combinations. A-B, A-C, and A-D sheets are useful and economical. They work best where only the good side will be visible.

Shop grade plywood may be any of the other face grades, rejected for a split or a glue failure. This inexpensive grade is fine for woodworking projects if you cut out or hide the defective areas.

The most common thicknesses for softwood plywood are ¼, ⅜, ½, ⅝, and ¾ inch.

Hardwood plywood. Hardwood plywoods, more expensive than softwood types, are an economical alternative to solid hardwoods. Ash and birch are popular choices, but other domestic and imported types are available.

Hardwood plywood, like softwood plywood, receives a separate rating for each face. Premium grade, the best, has well-matched veneers (surface layers) and uniform color; Good grade veneers are not as well matched. Sound grade is not uniform in color, but has no open defects.

Premium grade is suitable for a natural finish, as are some Good grade veneers. In general, though, Good grade looks best when stained. Sound grade should be painted for best appearance.

Hardwood plywood is available in thicknesses of ⅛, 3⁄16, ¼, ⅜, ½, ⅝, ¾, and 1 inch.

Plywood edges. The inner veneers of some plywood grades may have voids, which can be unsightly if the edges will be exposed. You can solve this problem by covering the edges with paint, veneer, or molding.

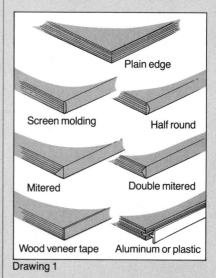

Plain edge
Screen molding
Half round
Mitered
Double mitered
Wood veneer tape
Aluminum or plastic

Drawing 1

Another solution is to buy solid-core sheets. Made of face veneers glued to a solid core, this kind of plywood has easily worked edges. You might also try Finnish or Baltic plywood, a birch plywood made up of many very thin, solid veneers. Exposed edges of this plywood have a handsome, finished appearance.

Measuring & marking

Once you've chosen your materials, you'll have to measure and mark them for cutting. For this, you'll need a measuring tool, a straightedge, a square, and something to mark with.

Measuring tools

Tight-fitting joinery for projects such as cabinets demands measuring and cutting to within 1/32 or 1/64 inch. Less "critical" pieces, such as bookshelf boards, can be cut to within 1/16 inch. For rough measuring, you can use a wooden yardstick or ruler. For more precise work, use a steel tape measure, a bench rule, or the blade of a square. Whenever possible, use one board to transfer measurements to another (see Drawing 1). No matter what tools you use, always measure twice before you cut.

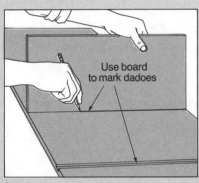

Drawing 1

Bench rule. Made of steel or wood, the bench rule, 1 to 3 feet long, may be marked in increments of 1/8, 1/16, 1/32, 1/64, 1/10, and 1/100 inch. This rules provides a firm straightedge to mark against. For greatest accuracy, measure from an inside mark, not the end.

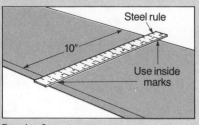

Drawing 2

Steel tape measure. For longer measurements, use a flexible steel tape—the longer and wider the better.

A tape measure's end hook should be riveted loosely, so that it will adjust for precise inside and outside measurements. The case should be an even 2 or 3 inches long for accurate inside measurements. Most tapes are marked at 1/16 and 1/32-inch increments.

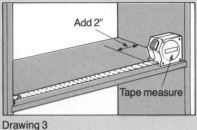

Drawing 3

Combination square. The blade of a combination square excels for making precise, short measurements, as well as for marking 90° and 45° angles. It's marked in increments of 1/16, 1/32, and 1/64 inch. This tool's versatility allows it to do several jobs (see drawing below).

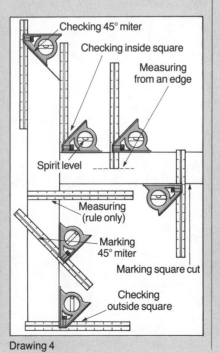

Drawing 4

Carpenter's square. When a combination square is too small, use this 16 by 24-inch square—normally a carpenter's framing and planning tool—for laying out lines and checking for square. The blades may be marked in increments of 1/8, 1/16, and 1/32 inch.

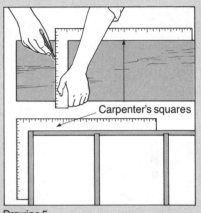

Drawing 5

Sliding T-bevel. The adjustable T-bevel is commonly used for transferring fixed angles between 0° and 180° from piece to piece. Its blade can be set for any angle with the aid of a protractor, though some T-bevels have angles marked on the face.

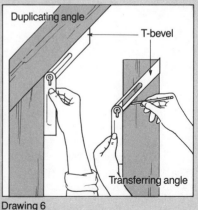

Drawing 6

Compass or wing dividers. A simple schoolroom compass draws circles or arcs and also works for limited measuring jobs. Wing dividers are more precise (they have a knurled, locking screw that holds the legs in place), but also more expensive. Use them to transfer small measurements.

For curves and circles with large radiuses, tack one end of a thin strip of wood or a yardstick to the material to be marked, hold a pencil against the strip or yardstick at the desired radius, and pivot.

Marking lines accurately

Laying out most projects will require marking lines—some straight, some curved, some at a particular angle. The first tool you'll need for this is a steel scribe, a sharp utility knife, or a good sharp pencil. A scribe or knife marks a more precise line than a pencil, but it leaves an indelible mark (pencil lines can be erased).

For accurate pencil lines and markings tilt the pencil, scribe, or knife so the point is as close as possible to the straightedge (see Drawing 7). When measuring a board for a cut, first mark the line's position, then draw it so its thickness lies outside the measured area (on the "waste" side of the board).

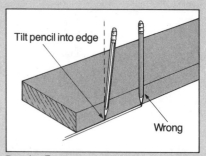

Tilt pencil into edge

Wrong

Drawing 7

Sawing

Sawing is an integral part of all woodworking projects—so it's important to choose the right saw for the job. The information below will help you select an appropriate saw for each cutting task and provide you with tips on using saws successfully. Be sure to protect your eyes when using a power saw.

Making a clean cut

The number of teeth per inch along a saw blade determines the kind of cut it makes. The more numerous the teeth, the smoother the cut. Use handsaws with about eight teeth per inch (TPI) for rough rips and crosscuts. Fine cuts for joinery are made with saws having a TPI of at least 12. For a power saw, you can choose blades specifically intended for the cuts you need to make.

Wood tends to splinter and break away where saw teeth exit. The saw you use determines what side of the wood splinters. Cut with the good side of the wood facing *up* when using a handsaw, table saw, or radial-arm saw. If you use a portable circular saw or saber saw, cut the wood with the good side facing *down*.

To minimize splintering, score along the back side of the cutting line. Or try taping the line's back side with masking tape. Better yet, back the cut by clamping another piece of wood against the piece you're cutting, then cut both pieces together.

If you're cutting a large piece of wood, always support both segments. Otherwise, the saw may bind, and the unsupported piece will break away. If the saw binds anyway, wedge a screwdriver blade in the end of the cut to open it.

Sawing straight lines

You can cut straight lines with several kinds of saws: handsaw, saber saw, portable circular saw, table saw, and radial-arm saw.

Regardless of the saw you use, the secret of cutting straight is using a guide. Table saws and radial-arm saws have built-in guides, but if you use a hand-held saw, improvise a guide (see Drawing 1) or use a guide attachment.

Handsaw. Guide a handsaw against a board clamped along the cutting line. Start a cut by drawing the saw up slowly a few times to make a notch or "kerf." Making a full kerf about ½ inch into the board's far edge will help to guide the blade straight for the rest of the cut. Then saw with short strokes at the blade's wide end, progressing to smooth, long, generous strokes. Keep your forearm in line with the blade. Saw lumber at a 45° angle; cut plywood and other sheet materials at 30° (see Drawing 1).

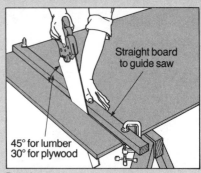

Straight board to guide saw

45° for lumber
30° for plywood

Drawing 1

Saber saw. A saber saw usually comes with a guide designed for making straight cuts a short distance from, and parallel to, a board's edge (see Drawing 2). When cutting across panels or wide surfaces, guide the saw's base plate against a straightedge clamped a measured distance from the cutting line. Keep the saw firmly against the guide

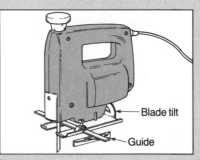

Blade tilt

Guide

Drawing 2

and check the blade continually to see that it doesn't bend away from the cut; it should stay vertically straight.

Portable circular saws. Like saber saws, circular saws come with guides for ripping narrow widths. For cutting large panels, use a guide like that shown in Drawing 1 on the facing page.

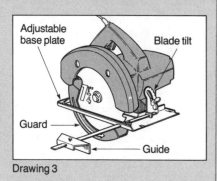
Drawing 3

Table saw and radial-arm saw. The table saw and the radial-arm saw are both stationary power saws. They're accurate tools that can perform other woodworking operations besides cutting (consult your owner's manual).

The table saw is a circular saw that's permanently mounted in a table (see Drawing 4). The blade is stationary—instead of moving the blade through the wood, you feed the wood to the blade. Locking rip fences (bars that clamp across the table) and miter gauges (guides that run in slots in the table) make the table saw an accurate saw for ripping or for crosscutting shorter pieces of wood. (Long lengths can be crosscut with this saw, too, but they can be awkward to handle.) Combination blades are available for general-purpose work; you can also change the blade to suit particular jobs.

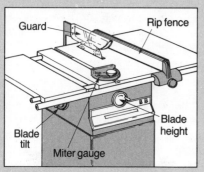
Drawing 4

The radial-arm saw, another circular saw, uses the same blade types as the portable circular saw and table saw. The wood is positioned on a table; the motor and blade, mounted on an arm above the table, are drawn across (see Drawing 5). The saw can be raised, lowered, tilted, and even swiveled for miter cuts or rip cuts. It has several advantages over the table saw: it crosscuts long pieces easily, it's convenient for making miter cuts, and it adapts readily to many other woodworking operations.

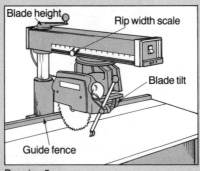
Drawing 5

Sawing curves & irregular lines

Blades for sawing curves, zigzags, and irregular cuts must be thin and narrow. They're used in an almost straight-up-and-down position relative to the surface. The keyhole saw, coping saw, and saber saw are suitable for this kind of cutting.

Keyhole saw. This hand-powered version of the saber saw (see Drawing 6) cuts curves and cutouts in the centers of panels (start from a drilled hole).

Drawing 6

Coping saw. The coping saw, limited by its metal frame, cuts tightly curved or straight lines close to a board's edge (see Drawing 7). Its blade is removable. A coping saw is generally used with the teeth pointing away from the han-

dle, so cuts are made on the push stroke. But you may find the saw easier to use if you turn the blade around (teeth pointing toward the handle) so it cuts on the pull stroke, as illustrated.

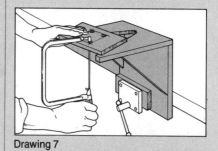
Drawing 7

Saber saw. The saber saw (see Drawing 2 on facing page) can do almost any kind of cutting, including curved lines. For greatest control, get a saber saw with a variable-speed trigger.

Cutting a miter

A miter is simply a through cut made at an angle. Mark the miter first, using a combination square or sliding T-bevel; then cut it just as you would cut straight across the board, but hold the saw at the desired angle. Use a backsaw and cut to the outside of the cutting line.

Radial-arm saws and table saws are excellent for cutting precise miters. When you set the blade of a radial-arm saw or the miter gauge of a table saw at the desired angle, you can easily make accurate miter cuts.

If you're cutting miters with a handsaw, a miter box will aid you enormously. It supports small pieces of wood securely and guides the saw for precise cuts at the desired angle (see Drawing 8).

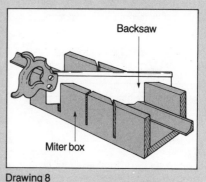
Drawing 8

Shaping & smoothing

Chisels, planes, abrasive tools, and routers, like saws, are essential tools for many woodworking operations. They're used for shaping and smoothing wood.

Chisels

Used primarily for cutting grooves and mortises, chisels come in a variety of blade widths and lengths. Shallow cuts can be made with any length of chisel; deep cuts, such as mortises, require long blades.

Always keep your chisels sharp. Whenever possible, cut with the grain and make shallow cuts. Generally, a chisel is used with the bevel *down* for roughing cuts, *up* for paring and finishing cuts.

The type of work you're doing also determines the position of the bevel. Cut inside curves and bottoms of deep recesses with the bevel down; cut outside curves and make open cuts with the bevel up (see Drawing 1).

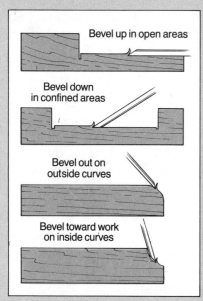

Drawing 1

Planes

These tools reduce widths and thicknesses, smooth surfaces and edges cut with other tools, square and true the edges of a piece of wood, and chamfer and bevel edges (see Drawing 2).

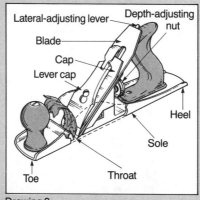

Drawing 2

Block plane. About 6 inches long, the block plane is suited for smoothing end grain and plywood edges, trimming the ends of moldings, and chamfering and beveling across the grain.

Smoothing plane. Woodworkers use this 9-inch-long plane for the final smoothing of a surface. Keep the blade razor sharp and properly adjusted to produce a thin shaving.

Jack plane. The jack plane is heavier than the smoothing plane; it's also longer (14 to 15 inches). It's generally used to smooth rough surfaces.

Jointer plane. This 22 to 24-inch-long plane produces the smoothest and flattest cut of any plane. Because of its length, it can span the valleys of an irregular surface, cutting down the high spots until the surface is smooth and flat. Use a jointer plane on boards that will be joined edge to edge.

Tips on using planes. Practice and experiment with your planes on scrap wood to develop your skills.

Always keep the plane blade sharp and adjust it so that the edge is parallel to the sole, producing a shaving of uniform thickness from side to side.

With the exception of the block plane, the planes described at left have a cap attached to the blade. This increases the curl of the shaving and breaks thicker ones. Adjust the position of the cap to leave 1/16 inch between the edge of the cap and the edge of the blade, keeping the edges parallel.

When planing, angle the plane slightly to the direction of travel (see Drawing 3) and move it forward smoothly. Apply uniform pressure except at the beginning and end of each pass: start with slightly more pressure on the toe than on the rest of the plane, and finish with slightly more pressure on the heel. To produce the smoothest surface, determine how the grain slopes and cut "uphill," as shown.

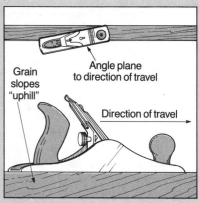

Drawing 3

Abrasive tools

Files and rasps are examples of abrasive tools. Use them to remove excess wood in small areas or to rough out shapes of larger areas. These tools are available in many styles, shapes, and degrees of coarseness.

Router

This versatile tool can give your projects a very finished look. Depending on the bit used, it can round, bevel, or otherwise shape the edge of a board; cut straight, V-shaped, and rounded grooves; and shave wood to smooth it.

Drilling holes

If a woodworking project requires you to join two or more pieces of wood, it often involves drilling holes. Your choice of cutting tools for hole-drilling will depend on several factors: the hole size, the degree of accuracy necessary in the hole's placement, and whether you'll turn the cutting tool by hand or power.

Drills & bits

Some are called drills, some are called bits, and some are called augers, but all cut holes in wood. Attach them to your hand or power drill, choosing the type best suited to your needs. Those most useful to the woodworker are described below (see Drawing 1).

Twist drills. Though intended for drilling holes in metal, twist drills can also drill holes in wood. Fractional, number, and letter-size twist bits cover a wide range of sizes and can be used with both hand and power drills.

Augers. Typically used with a bit brace, the auger is a centuries-old standby for drilling holes in wood. For clean, accurate holes, use the double-twist variety, which has two spurs and a screw lead. For harder woods and for very deep holes, a solid-center auger is best. Auger bits are commonly available in sizes ranging from ¼ to 1½ inches, in ¹⁄₁₆-inch increments.

Brad point drills. Also known as woodbit drills, these drill round, clean holes and don't "wander" when you start them. They're available in sizes from ⅛ to ½ inch (in ¹⁄₁₆-inch increments), for use with both hand and power drills.

Forstner bits. These bits cut accurate, clean-sided, flat-bottomed holes.

Because the bit is guided by the edge of the tool instead of the center, you can bore the arc of a circle in any direction, regardless of the wood grain. These features can help you make oval and curved openings. Forstner bits are for

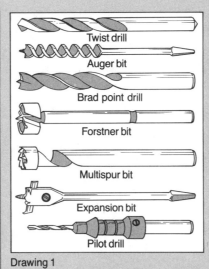

Drawing 1

Twist drill
Auger bit
Brad point drill
Forstner bit
Multispur bit
Expansion bit
Pilot drill

use only with power drills; they're available in sizes from ¼ to 2 inches, in ⅛-inch increments.

Multispur bits. These bits don't wander when you start the drill, won't get clogged with wood chips, and can drill the arc of a circle without splitting the wood. They'll also cut through veneered stock without tearing it. Available in 17 sizes (from ½ to 2⅛ inches), they're for use in power drills.

Expansion bits. Expansion bits, used with bit braces, are available in two adjustable sizes. One size can be adjusted from ⅝ to 1¾ inches, the other from ⅞ to 3 inches.

Pilot drills. A number of pilot drill systems for woodscrews are available. In one operation, a pilot drill cuts the proper size holes for the threads and shank of a screw—then countersinks the hole so the screw head is flush, or counterbores a hole that can be plugged to hide the screw head. You can buy pilot drills in sizes appropriate for #6, #8, #10, and #12 woodscrews.

Drilling properly

While you're drilling, wear plastic safety goggles to protect your eyes from wood chips and sawdust. Clamp materials down, particularly when using a power drill. Hold the drill firmly.

If your bit doesn't have a screw or brad point lead, a couple of taps with a hammer on a large nail, nailset, or punch will leave a hole that will prevent the bit from wandering when you start to drill.

When possible, adapt the drill speed to the size of the hole you're drilling. The smaller the drill bit, the higher the speed. Use light pressure, letting the bit do the work; excessive pressure and speed overheat and ruin bits.

To avoid breaking small bits, don't tilt the drill once it has entered the wood. Leave the motor on as you remove the bit from the wood.

Unless you have a drill press or a press accessory for your power drill, drilling straight holes may be difficult. Three methods you can try are shown below (see Drawing 2).

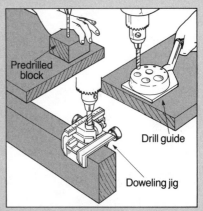

Predrilled block
Drill guide
Doweling jig

Drawing 2

To drill a hole to a specific depth, you can mark the depth on the bit with masking tape, use a predrilled block of wood as a depth gauge, or buy a commercial depth stop.

When you're drilling through a piece of wood, keep the back side from breaking away by doing one of two things: 1) lay or clamp a piece of wood firmly against your work piece's back side and drill through the work piece into the wood; or 2) just before the drill pierces, flip the work piece over and finish drilling from the other side.

Joinery

Joinery is the craft of putting pieces of wood together securely so that the joints can't move or come apart. It's the most varied aspect of woodworking, as well as the most demanding—fitting pieces accurately and securely determines the success of your project.

Basic joints

The following guide to the most commonly used joints explains the use and construction of each one.

Butt joints. These are the easiest joints to make (see Drawing 1). First, square off the end of one board and butt the end against the other board. Glue and clamp; then add screws or nails.

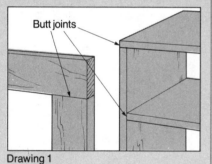

Drawing 1

Butt joints are fairly weak unless reinforced with dowels, corner blocks (see page 90), special fasteners, or brackets.

Miter joints. Two pieces cut at an angle and joined at the ends make up a miter joint (see Drawing 2). These joints are used for trim and for hiding end grain. They're not strong, but they can

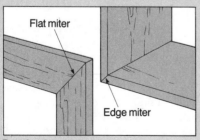

Drawing 2

be reinforced with dowels, splines (see page 90), brackets, or nails. There are two kinds of miters: flat and edge.

Flat miters are easiest to make. When you're using hand tools to cut the wood, these miters are most accurately cut with a miter box. (Or mark the angles with a combination square and then cut carefully, using a wood strip as a guide.) Table and radial-arm saws have adjustable guides that make mitering a simple technique.

Edge miters are best made with a table or radial-arm saw. They're difficult to cut with hand tools: wide stock won't fit in most miter boxes, and it's tricky to cut with a tilted handsaw.

Rabbet joints. Rabbets are cut along board edges; the mating piece rests within the rabbet, as shown in Drawing 3.

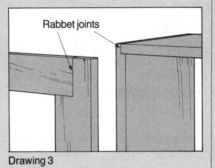

Drawing 3

Rabbets are used at corners and for recessing back panels. They help cut down visible end and edge grain, and because of the extra surface area they offer for gluing, they're strong.

Cutting a rabbet with hand tools is a bit difficult—the goal is to make cuts as perpendicular to the board surfaces as possible. A backsaw or dovetail saw, some type of vise or clamp, and a scrap of wood as a guide will help you do the job.

First, use a combination square to mark out lines on the end, face, and two edges (see Drawing 4). Cut to the point where the end cut will intersect the face cut. The end cut is tricky: there's

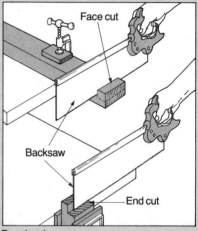

Drawing 4

no good way to clamp on a guide. Saw down carefully to meet the face cut. Clean and finish the rabbet with a chisel and sandpaper.

Portable power tools make cutting rabbets easier. It's quickest to use a router equipped with a self-guiding rabbet bit. If you have a circular saw, set it to the desired depth and cut along the face line first. Then reset the saw depth and make the end cut.

Dado joints. While rabbets are made along a board's end or edge, dadoes are usually cross-grain grooves across a board's edge or face. Like rabbet joints, dado joints are strong; they're widely used to join horizontal pieces to uprights as in cabinets and bookcases.

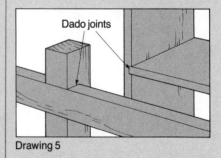

Drawing 5

To make a dado, first draw the border lines across the board, using the piece for the other part of the joint as a guide (see page 83). Then extend the lines around the edges, using a combination square, and connect the two edge lines at the proper depth. Now the dado is mapped out.

Power tools are best for dadoes. The router, equipped with a straight bit, smooths the cut as it goes (clamp on a guide for the router base to follow).

To cut dadoes with a power saw blade, set the blade at the right depth, cut the borders (using a guide), and make repeated passes through the waste wood until it virtually falls out. Dress each groove with light chisel strokes. (You can also buy dado blades for both power saws and portable saws; these blades can cut a dado in one pass.)

To cut a dado with hand tools, clamp a straight piece of wood along one face line as a guide, then cut to the right depth (see Drawing 6). Move the guide to the other face line and repeat. Make extra saw cuts through the waste area; this technique makes it easier to chisel out the waste, resulting in a more uniform bottom for the dado.

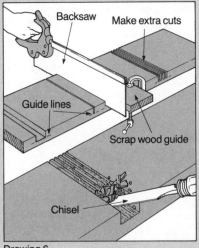

Drawing 6

Use a chisel to remove any remaining wood. First position chisel with the bevel down and tap lightly with a hammer or mallet; then turn chisel so bevel is up and smooth out the groove with hand pressure.

Lap joints. Overlapping construction often involves use of lap joints. Dadoes or rabbets are cut in two pieces; then, the pieces are overlapped and fastened together.

There are three types of lap joints: cross-lap, end-lap, and half-lap (see Drawing 7). Each can be cut with hand tools, power saws, or with a router and a straight or rabbet bit.

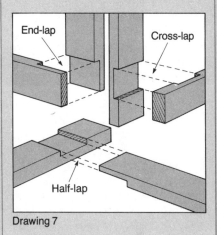

Drawing 7

Cross-lap joints are relatively easy to make. The width of each dado should be exactly the same as the width of the connecting piece; the depth of each dado should be one-half the thickness of the connecting piece. Refer to "Dado joints," page 88, for information on cutting with hand tools, a router, or power saws.

End-lap joints are made up of two rabbet cuts that fit together (see "Rabbet joints," page 88). The depth of each cut should be one-half the thickness of the boards.

A half-lap joint is a combination of a cross lap and an end lap and is cut as described above for those two joints.

Mortise and tenon joints. One of the stronger joints for joining two pieces of wood at a right angle, the mortise and tenon joint (see Drawing 8) exists in dozens of varieties.

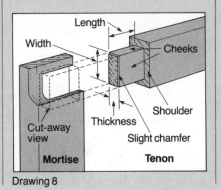

Drawing 8

These joints can be made in several ways. Described below is a method for cutting either through or blind joints using hand tools; you can adapt this technique to other types of mortise and tenon joints. If you own a router or a table or radial-arm saw, check your owner's manual for instructions. Practice on scrap wood until you become proficient.

Most woodworkers cut the mortise first: if something goes wrong with it, you can simply enlarge it and then cut the tenon to fit.

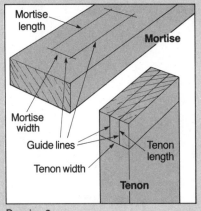

Drawing 9

Mark the mortise as shown in Drawing 9. Using an auger, brad point, or Forstner bit, drill a series of holes the same diameter as the width of the mortise, making sure the holes are perpendicular. For an open mortise, drill all the way through the piece; for a closed one, drill to the depth required. Chisel out excess material (see Drawing 10).

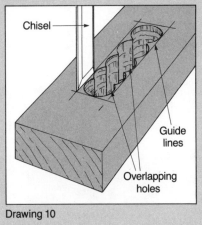

Drawing 10

Pare the opening to the marked lines, making the corners square and the sides perpendicular. For the ends of the mortise, use a chisel slightly narrower than the width of the mortise; use a wide chisel on the sides or cheeks.

Mark the cuts on the sides of the tenon as shown in Drawing 9 on page 89; repeat for the narrow sides of the tenon. Mark the tenon a little longer than necessary; you can cut it to length later.

To cut the tenon, first make the shoulder cuts with a backsaw (see Drawing 11). You can clamp a wood block to the piece to guide the cut, as shown.

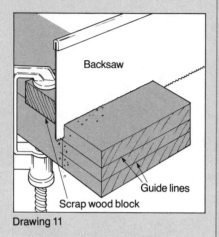
Drawing 11

The cheek cuts can be made in two ways. To use the first technique, make a series of saw cuts along the cheeks to the same depth as the shoulder cuts; then chisel away the excess material. Or follow the second method: Clamp the work in a vise with the tenon end up. Then use a backsaw to cut along the guidelines marking the cheeks until the kerfs meet the shoulder cuts (see Drawing 12).

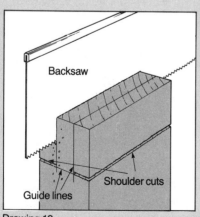
Drawing 12

The tenon should fit snugly in the mortise without being forced. Make any adjustments in small steps, using a chisel and sandpaper and making sure that the cheeks of the tenon are smooth.

Cut the tenon to length, 1/16 inch shorter than the depth of the mortise for a closed joint. Chamfer the end of the tenon as shown in Drawing 8 on page 89.

Reinforcement

The three reinforcements described below help strengthen joints.

Dowels. Dowels don't make joints—they reinforce them. For "through" doweling (see Drawing 13), you insert dowels all the way through one or both of the pieces to be joined.

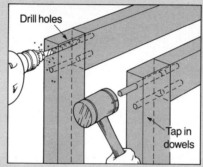
Drawing 13

For "blind" doweling (see Drawing 14), dowels are inserted part way through both pieces.

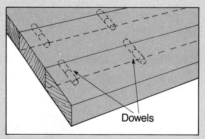
Drawing 14

For either kind of doweling, choose a drill bit the same diameter as the dowel. A doweling jig (see Drawing 15) will help you drill straight, accurate holes. (See page 87 for tips on drilling.) Cut small lengthwise grooves in the sides of the dowel to allow excess glue to escape;

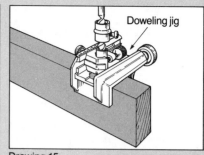
Drawing 15

then coat the dowel with glue and tap it in place with a mallet or light hammer.

Drill the holes for through dowels with the pieces clamped together. Sand the dowel ends smooth, or recess them and cover with plugs (see page 94).

When you blind-dowel two pieces together, you insert the dowels in separate, matching holes drilled in the touching faces of the two pieces to be joined (see Drawing 14). When the joint is completed, the dowels don't show on the project's surface.

There are two basic ways to blind-dowel a joint. You can lay the two surfaces side by side and mark them as shown (see Drawing 16), then tip them on edge and drill both holes slightly deeper than half the dowel length. Or you can try a second method: drill one hole, insert a dowel center in the hole, and press the pieces together. The dowel center will mark where the second hole must be drilled.

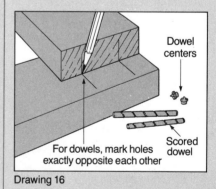
Drawing 16

Corner blocks. Also known as glue blocks, corner blocks are triangular or squared strips of wood glued along the inside edges of joints.

Wooden splines. These are sometimes inserted in grooves cut in the

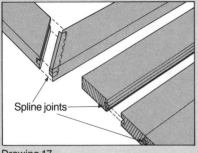

Spline joints

Drawing 17

mating edges of boards, both as a means of positioning the pieces and reinforcing the joints (see Drawing 17).

Since splines demand accurate cutting, it's best to cut them with power tools—though you can use a backsaw or dovetail saw if you wish. To be sure each set of grooves will match, use the same table saw or router setting to cut each one.

The width of the spline should be slightly less than the combined depth of the two grooves. A ¼-inch-thick, 1¼-inch-wide spline is a good size for most work. The most convenient material to use for splines is ¼-inch plywood.

Once you've cut the spline, spread glue along one side and place it in one of the grooves. Then spread glue along the other side of the spline, push the other piece into place, and clamp. When the glue is dry, trim the spline ends flush; sand the surfaces smooth.

Drawers

Drawers can expand storage capacity immensely. You may be able to buy premade drawers in standard sizes at home-improvement centers and design cabinets to fit them. But it's less expensive and more challenging—and not too difficult—to make your own drawers. In addition, you'll be assured of getting exactly the drawer you need. You can construct drawers using either hand or power tools.

Materials

You can use hardboard for drawer bottoms; it's thin (only ¼ inch thick), but rigid and strong. For the sides, fronts, and backs, you can use solid wood or plywood. Since solid wood may tend to warp, you may want to use it simply as an attractive finish for drawer fronts (see Drawing 1). Plywood resists warping, and it's strong for its weight.

Whether you're using solid wood or plywood, you can use ¾-inch stock for drawer fronts and ½, ⅝, or ¾-inch stock for sides and backs. If you plan to cut dadoes for the bottom or for runners, choose ⅝ or ¾-inch-thick wood for the drawer sides.

Using hand tools

A drawer built with hand tools is essentially a specialized box, made with butt joints for ease of assembly (see Drawing 1). To put it together, you'll need a crosscut saw, nails, a hammer, a tape measure, clamps, and glue.

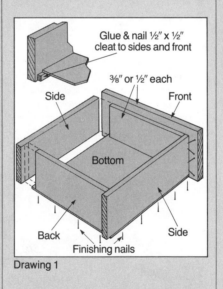

Glue & nail ½" x ½" cleat to sides and front

⅜" or ½" each

Side

Front

Bottom

Back

Side

Finishing nails

Drawing 1

Cut the pieces to the required sizes and check for square. Glue and nail the two front panels together; then attach the two sides to the inside front panel. Next, fit the back between the sides and glue and nail it in place.

Flip the assembly upside down and square it up with a combination square. Then attach the bottom to the sides, back, and inside front panel. If you want to reinforce the bottom, cut it to fit inside the drawer and attach cleats, as shown. Then glue and nail the bottom to the tops of the cleats. Clamp the joints so they'll dry square.

Using power tools

By building a drawer with power tools, you can take advantage of the more sophisticated joinery techniques these tools make possible. The drawer shown in Drawing 2 requires rabbets and dadoes (see pages 88–89). You'll need a power saw, a router, nails, a hammer, a tape measure, clamps, and glue.

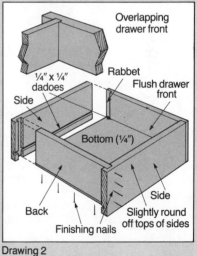

Overlapping drawer front

¼" x ¼" dadoes

Rabbet

Flush drawer front

Side

Bottom (¼")

Back

Finishing nails

Side

Slightly round off tops of sides

Drawing 2

Cut the pieces to the required sizes and check for square. Cut rabbets and dadoes in the front and sides, as shown.

Glue and nail the sides to the front. Next, slip the back piece between the sides, check for square, and glue and nail through each side into the back.

Slide the bottom into the ¼-inch dadoes in the sides and front, then nail through the bottom into the back with a few small nails. This way the bottom "floats," with room to swell and contract.

Drawer guides

Lightweight drawers that aren't too wide can slide in and out without guides. But wide or heavy drawers should have guides of some type. Since drawer measurements may have to be altered to accommodate the type of guides in-stalled, always decide on the guides you'll use before building the drawer.

Manufactured metal guides or slides are the smoothest and easiest to work with; they're also the most expensive. Install these according to manufacturer's directions.

Several different types of wood or plastic guides are shown in Drawing 3. The plastic channel can be bought at a home improvement center. You can make the other guides using wood strips (see pages 88–89 for information on cutting dadoes and rabbets).

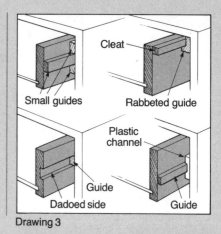
Drawing 3

Hinged doors

Hinged doors fall into three categories: flush, overlapping, and lip (see Drawing 1). Sliding doors, not discussed here, follow grooved tracks.

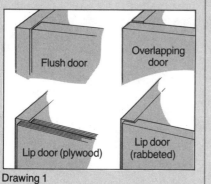
Drawing 1

Flush doors are set inside the edges of a unit. Overlapping doors sit in front of a unit; they're easy to install and more forgiving of errors in alignment. Lip doors are similar, but the inside edges are grooved (rabbeted) to inset slightly. You can also fashion a lip by gluing a smaller plywood piece on the back face of an overlapping door.

Drop doors (such as on cabinets or wall-mounted shelves) open by swinging down. With proper support (stay supports or chains), they can double as table or desk surfaces. Drop doors may be flush, overlapping, or lip.

Hinges

Hinges are available in hundreds of shapes and sizes (see Drawing 2).

Butt hinges are used for flush doors and doors that fully overlap the front of the cabinet. Those with removable pins allow you to remove the door without unscrewing the hinges.

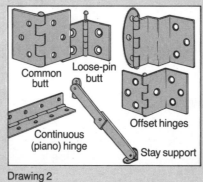
Drawing 2

Offset hinges are designed for flush, partially overlapping, and lip doors; they also help you avoid having to fasten into the edges of plywood doors.

Continuous hinges (piano hinges) are best for drop doors; they can be used for any flush door, as well. These hinges are available in lengths up to 6 feet; cut them to exact size with a hacksaw.

Stay supports are helpful for pre-venting drop doors from opening too far, and enable the opened doors to be used as desks or work surfaces.

Installing hinged doors

To fit properly in door openings, flush and lip doors must be cut accurately, allowing 1/16-inch clearance between the edge of the door and the cabinet on all four sides.

Flush-mounted doors are installed with offset, continuous, or butt hinges. Usually these are mortised into the edge of the door and the cabinet so that most of the hinge is hidden. Center the door in the opening and hold it in place with small wood wedges; then mark the hinge locations a fourth of the way down from the top of the door and a fourth of the way up from the bottom. Cut the mortises; screw the hinges to the door, then to the cabinet.

Full overlapping doors are mounted with butt or continuous hinges mortised into the back of the door and the face of the cabinet.

Hinges for lip and overlapping doors are easier to install if you place the cabinet on its back. Attach the hinges to the back of the door (some may require a mortise); then position the door over the opening and screw the hinges to the cabinet.

Fastening

Wood joints may be secured with fasteners, glue, or a combination of the two. Gluing a properly designed joint creates the strongest bond. But you may find it easier to make joints if you use both glue and some kind of fastener: in effect, the fastener acts as a permanent clamp.

Nails

The easiest way to join two pieces of wood is to nail them together. The resulting joint is neither the strongest nor the cleanest one you can make—but it is the simplest. Nails hold wood by friction, making a joint that's fairly strong if no direct pressure is exerted to pull it apart.

Nail types. Box and finishing nails are best for woodworking. Box nails have wide, flat heads. When you don't want nails to show, use finishing nails: they have slender heads that you can hammer in, then recess by setting (countersinking) with a tap on a tool called a nailset. After you fill the resulting hole and sand the surface smooth, the nails will be invisible from the outside.

Choose a nail two to three times as long as the thickness of the top piece of material to be joined. Whenever possible, nail through the thinner into the thicker piece of material.

Both box and finishing nails come in sizes from 2 to 60-penny. "Penny" (abbreviated as "d") once referred to the cost of 100 hand-forged nails; 16-penny nails, for instance, were 16 cents per hundred. Nail diameter increases with increasing penny measurement, as does nail length: a 2d nail is 1 inch long, while a 60d nail has a length of 6 inches.

Nailing techniques. Sharp nail tips split wood easily. Before driving them, blunt them with a few hammer taps.

To start a nail, hold it just below the head, between your thumb and forefinger; give it a few light hammer taps to get it going. (Holding the nail this way protects your fingers: if you miss the nail, you'll knock your fingers out of the way rather than smashing them.) Once the nail is started, you can let go of it and use harder hammer strokes.

Keep the hammer face parallel to the nail head. Don't hit finishing nails full force on the last few swings—tap the nail nearly flush and then drive it 1/16 inch below the surface with a nailset.

Nails hold much better when driven at a slight angle. Don't place nails along the same grain line, since this tends to split the wood; stagger them instead. If nails are causing recurrent splitting, drill small pilot holes for them, especially in hard woods or at the ends of boards.

If you have a problem with a bent nail, remove the offender by gripping it with the claw of your hammer and rocking the hammer back. Larger nails come out more easily if bent to the side and "curled out." To protect the work surface or to provide more leverage, put a piece of scrap between the hammerhead and the work surface.

Brads. For very fine finishing work or for nailing into delicate edges, try brads. These fasteners are similar to finishing nails, but thinner. They're sized by length and wire gauge (a measure of diameter): the higher the number, the thinner the brad.

Screws

Though more time-consuming to drive than nails, screws make far stronger joints, especially when combined with glue. (Screwed joints without glue are preferable if you want to be able to disassemble the project.)

Screw types. The five kinds of screws commonly used in wood are illustrated in Drawing 1. Most common is the flathead, which sits flush with the material's surface. Flathead Phillips screws have heads notched in a crosslike pattern, to keep screwdrivers from slipping.

Two other common screws are the roundhead and the ovalhead. A roundhead screw's head sits atop the work surface; an ovalhead is partly recessed. Woodworkers use roundheads in thin wood or to attach thin material to a thicker piece of wood. Ovalheads are good for attaching exposed hardware; they can also serve as decoration, especially when installed with finishing washers.

The fifth type of screw, the lag screw (or lag bolt), is an oversize screw with a square or hexagonal head. Lag screws are driven with a wrench. They serve the same functions as woodscrews, but are used with larger pieces of wood.

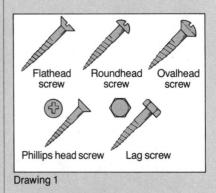

Flathead screw · Roundhead screw · Ovalhead screw · Phillips head screw · Lag screw

Drawing 1

Screw sizes. Woodscrews are sized by length (from 1/4 to 4 inches) and by wire gauge number (a measure of diameter). Numbers range from 0 to 24—about 1/16 to 3/8 inch.

Lag screws, with shafts ranging from 1/4 to 1/2 inch in diameter, come in lengths from 1 1/2 to 12 inches

Choose a screw two to three times the length of the top piece's thickness. Whenever possible, screw through the thinner into the thicker piece.

Driving screws. Screws usually require predrilled "pilot" holes in all but the softest materials. Pick a drill bit the diameter of the screw's shank (the part without threads) and drill only as deep as the length of the shank. In harder woods, also drill a smaller hole for the threads below the shank hole; it should be about half as deep as the threaded portion is long. Use a drill bit with a slightly smaller diameter than the core between the screw's threads.

Flathead screws are usually countersunk to sit flush with the wood surface. This requires drilling a tapered hole, the diameter and depth of the screw head, at the open end of the shank hole. The right size countersink bit for a brace or an electric or hand drill will make a hole that matches the tapered contour of the screw head.

A drill accessory called a pilot drill makes pilot and countersink holes simultaneously (see page 87). Some pilot drills are adjustable; others come in sets of individually sized bits.

You can also drive woodscrews beneath the surface by counterboring instead of countersinking, then covering the heads with plugs. Use a plug cutter (see Drawing 2) to cut the plugs—and make them from the same type of wood as the surface, so the grain and color will match.

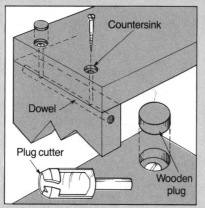

Drawing 2

For strength, use longer screws in end grain; or insert a dowel as shown in Drawing 2, then screw into that.

To drive lag screws, first drill a pilot hole with a bit two-thirds the diameter and length of the screw. Then drill a hole for the shank through the top piece. Start the screw by tapping it with a hammer, and finish driving it with an adjustable wrench. Lag screws are commonly fitted with washers beneath the head to distribute pressure and protect the surface below.

If a screw is stubborn when you try to drive it, try rubbing soap or wax on the threads. If it still sticks, drill a larger or longer pilot hole.

Glues

Combined with the right clamping technique, the right glue makes a much stronger joint than fasteners alone, and it doesn't mar the work surface.

White (polyvinyl) glue. The standard household glue, this works well on wood if the pieces are firmly clamped while the glue dries. White glue isn't waterproof, but it resists grease and solvents. Don't use it near high heat.

Aliphatic resin glue. This cream colored glue is stronger than white glue: it can make a joint stronger than the wood itself. It has a high resistance to heat and solvents, but it's not waterproof.

Waterproof glue. The most common waterproof glue for woodworking is plastic resin glue. Plastic resin bonds chemically, like epoxy, but requires clamping. It leaves a dark stain that will show through transparent finishes, so work carefully if you're planning a fine finish.

Clamps

Clamps serve two related purposes: they're like a second pair of hands helping to steady parts that are being assembled, and they hold joined pieces together while glue dries.

Clamps come in many shapes (see Drawing 3). You can also (and may sometimes have to) improvise your own.

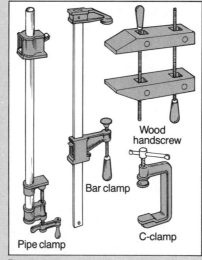

Wood handscrew

Bar clamp

Pipe clamp

C-clamp

Drawing 3

C-clamps. These are best for small jobs: clamping localized areas, holding work to a bench, and attaching wood guides for sawing. Maximum capacity ranges from 1 to 8 inches.

Wood handscrews. Handscrews can apply pressure over a large area; they're good for clamping nonparallel surfaces. Their wooden jaws adjust for depth and angles as well as width. Handscrew capacities range from 2 to 12 inches.

Bar clamps. Made in various sizes, bar clamps extend over long distances—up to 5 feet. Use bar clamps for holding together large units and series of more than one joint. They're also useful for joining wide boards at the edges.

Pipe clamps. Pipe clamps are a less expensive alternative to bar clamps. You buy the fittings and attach them to a length of pipe that suits your job.

Gluing & clamping

Before gluing, test the fit of the pieces to be glued by assembling them dry. Plan the assembly sequence in advance.

Make sure all the pieces you plan to glue are clean and dry. Spread glue thinly and evenly on both surfaces to be joined to within about 1/16 inch of the edge. (The end grain of wood is usually quite porous and may absorb extra glue, so give it two coats.) If you're using a fast-drying glue, be careful that glue applied to one part of a large surface doesn't dry while you're working on another area.

Most glues allow for some adjustment of pieces during assembly. Check joint angles with a combination square and adjust before the glue sets. Temporary wood braces can be tacked on to fix angles.

When clamping, cushion the clamp jaws with pieces of wood, cardboard, or rubber to avoid marring the work surface. Tighten clamps until snug, but not too tight; you don't want to squeeze all the glue out of the joint.

If you plan to paint the piece, remove excess glue with a damp cloth. For natural finishes, allow the glue to dry before chipping off excess with a chisel.

Finishing

A good finish keeps dirt and moisture out of wood pores, wards off dents and scratches, and enhances the appearance of fine wood.

Wood repairs

Cracks, hammer marks, and holes will leave unsightly blemishes on your project if they aren't filled before sanding. The patching material usually depends on the type of finish you'll apply.

For a natural or stained finish. Fill blemishes with wood putty or stick shellac (a product used by furniture restorers). Wood putty is spread with a putty knife; stick shellac is melted into the blemish.

Because wood putty does not dry with the same porosity as wood, it accepts stains differently. Choose a wood putty that matches the stained wood or use a colored stick shellac.

Before painting. Almost any patching material works under a painted surface. You can use wood putty, spackle, or a mixture of glue and sawdust.

Sanding

There are three stages of sanding: rough, preparatory, and finish. For the rough stage—sanding out major defects or smoothing very rough wood— use 80-grit sandpaper. Finer paper (120-grit) is appropriate at the middle or preparatory stage, when you're sanding out small defects or giving the wood a general smoothing. Use 180 to 220-grit to get a super-smooth surface at the finish stage.

When the surface is smooth, vacuum it or dust it off with a brush. Then wipe the surface with a rag moistened with mineral spirits.

Sealing

A sealer is often applied to sanded wood before the finish goes on. Its primary function is to reduce moisture absorption so that later finish coats will go on more evenly.

Shellac, diluted with alcohol, is often used as a sealer. A coat applied before staining will help prevent the stain from soaking into the wood grain unevenly.

Stains

The stains below aren't finishes. They're used for coloring wood, to make it look aged or similar to another type of wood. Stains can also mask minor defects.

Pigmented oil stains. These are made of finely ground color pigments (similar to those used in coloring paints) mixed in a solution with tung oil, linseed oil, turpentine, or naphtha. Pigmented oil stains are sold as "oil stains," "wood stains," "sealer stains," and (sometimes) "pigmented wiping stains."

Penetrating oil stains. These stains are often confused with pigmented oil stains on dealers' shelves. True penetrating oil stains are composed of oil-soluble dyes dissolved in a synthetic or natural oil-base liquid.

Water stains. Though brilliant in color and inexpensive, water stains tend to swell wood grain; they also dry very slowly. Before using a water stain, wet the wood lightly with warm water and allow it to dry; then sand swollen areas flush again. When you apply the stain, there won't be much swelling.

Clear finishes

Clear finishes include penetrating oil sealer, varnish, polyurethane, shellac, and lacquer.

Polyurethane penetrating oil sealer. This is the easiest clear finish to apply. Just brush it on, allow it to stand for half an hour, and wipe it off with a clean rag. The wood retains its natural feel, though the color may darken.

Varnish. You can buy flat, satin (or semigloss), and gloss varnishes. Two coats are usually sufficient. Between coats, use 400-grit wet-and-dry sandpaper to remove excess gloss.

For each coat, liberally apply varnish with a brush. Stroke first with the grain, then across; then smooth out with the grain one last time.

Polyurethane. A synthetic finish similar in appearance to varnish, polyurethane (also sold as urethane) is extremely durable, as well as water and heat resistant. It's available in gloss and satin finishes.

Shellac. This easy-to-apply finish has a warm, subtle tone. It's not resistant to water or solvents.

Lacquer. Lacquer is a fast-drying finish similar to shellac; it has good durability and hardness. The drying speed of this finish may be a liability, since it can dry before it's been smoothly brushed. Make sure the stain and sealer you use are compatible with lacquer.

Enamel paints

For bright, solid colors—and for masking lower grades of wood—choose an enamel paint. There are three types: oil-base, acrylic-base, and polyurethane. Each has certain advantages.

Oil-base enamel covers better than acrylic and is more durable. Acrylic-base (latex) dries quickly and cleans up with warm water. Polyurethane is the toughest of the three; use it for the greatest resistance to abrasion.

All three enamels are available in flat and semigloss appearances; oil-base and polyurethane are also available in gloss. Apply them with a brush, as you would varnish (see above).

If you're using enamel on bare wood, it's best to apply an undercoat to seal the wood before brushing on the finish coat. Sand the undercoat with 220-grit sandpaper; also lightly sand each finish coat but the final one.

Sunset
Proof-of-Purchase
0-376-04888-3

INDEX

Abrasive tools, 86
Aliphatic resin glue, 94
Augers, 87

Back-yard sandbox, 47
Bar clamps, 94
Bathroom fittings, 12
Beds, 38–39
Bench/planter, garden, 78–79
Bench rule, 83
Bird feeder, hanging, 74
Birdhouse, custom-made, 75
Bits & drills, 87
Blade rack, 8
Block plane, 86
Blocks, building, 47
Boat, one-passenger, 51
Boat, wind-up toy, 40
Bolted square table, 29
Bonum board, 65
Bookend, slide-on, 18
Book racks, 17, 18–19
Boxes, hanging, toy shelves in, 50
Boxes, tote, 10
Brad point drills, 87
Brads, 93
Building blocks, 47
Built-in wine rack, 15
Bunk beds, 39
Butcher block table, 31
Butt joints, 88

Cantilevered chair, 30
Carpenter's square, 83
Carryall, stepstool, 11
C-clamps, 94
Centipede racing clogs, 58
Chairs, 16–17, 22–25, 30, 53
Chest, child's storage, 48–49
Children's furniture & toys, 40–57
Child's storage chest, 48–49
Chisels, 86
Circular saws, portable, 85
Clamps, and clamping, 94
Clear finishes, 95
Clogs, centipede racing, 58
Coffee table, trompe l'oeil, 33
Combination square, 83
Compact table & stool set, 24–25
Compass, 83–84
Computer table, roll-around, 20–21
Cooling rack, 7
Coping saw, 85
Corner blocks, 90
Craft & hobby projects, 58–69
Custom-made birdhouse, 75

Dado joints, 88–89
Decorative mailbox, 72
Desk, small fry's, 42–43
Desk/drawing table, 61
Dimension lumber, buying, 81–82
Display case, 62–63
Doors, hinged, 92
Dowels, 90
Drawers, 91–92

Drawing table/desk, 61
Drills, and drilling, 87

Easy-to-make workbench, 59
Edges, plywood, 82
Enamel paints, 95
Expansion bits, 87

Fastening, 93–94
Finishes, and finishing, 95
Firewood box, 80
Flip ball, 64
Folding tables, 26–27
Folk toys, 64–65
Forstner bits, 87
Furniture projects, 20–39
  children's, 41–43, 48–50, 53

Garden & yard accessories, 70–80
Garden lights, 70
Garden planter, 77
  /bench, 78–79
  mini-, 79
Geometric wine rack, 14
Glass-topped table, 32
Glues, and gluing, 94
Gymnastic equipment, 68–69

Handsaw, 84
Handscrews, wood, 94
Hanging bird feeder, 74
Hanging plant shelf, 76
Hanging pot rack, 9
Hardwood plywood, buying, 82
Hinged doors, and hinges, 92
Hobby & craft projects, 58–69
Holes, drilling, 87
Hook, bathroom, 12
Horse swing, 44–45
Household accessories, 4–19
Housing, modular, 56

Jack plane, 86
Joinery, 88–91
Jointer plane, 86

Keyhole saw, 85
Knife rack, 8

Lacquer, 95
Lamp, reading, 13
Lanterns, outdoor, 71
Lap joints, 89
Lawn chair, 22–23
Lights, garden, 70
Lumber, dimension, buying, 81–82

Mailbox, decorative, 72
Mailbox & mirror, 11

Marking lines, techniques for, 84
Measuring tools, 83–84
Message center, 6
Mini-garden planter, 79
Mirror & mailbox, 11
Miter, cutting a, 85
Miter joints, 88
Modular housing, 56
Mortise and tenon joints, 89–90
Multispur bits, 87
Mural work table, 41

Nails, and nailing, 93
Napkin rings, 4

Oil stains, 95
One-passenger boat, 51
Outdoor lanterns, 71
Outdoor seat swing, 57
Oven rack push-pull, 9

Paints, enamel, 95
Paper holder, bathroom, 12
Patio table, 34
Peg racing, 64
Penetrating oil sealer, polyurethane, 95
Penetrating oil stains, 95
Pigmented oil stains, 95
Pilot drills, 87
Pipe clamps, 94
Planes, 86
Planes, scooter, 54–55
Plank & sawhorses, 60
Planter, garden, 77
  /bench, 78–79
  mini-, 79
Plant shelf, hanging, 76
Plant pot sleeves, 80
Play-block chairs & table, 53
Play center, 57
Playhouse, 52
Plywood, buying, 82
Polyurethane, 95
Polyurethane penetrating oil sealer, 95
Pot rack, hanging, 9
Push-pull, oven rack, 9

Rabbet joints, 88
Radial-arm saw, 85
Reading lamp, 13
Record rack, 18–19
Reinforcement, 90–91
Repairs, wood, 95
Ribbstol, Swedish, 69
Ring toss, 65
Roll-around computer table, 20–21
Rolling wood toy, 46
Router, 86
Rugged sawbuck, 72

Saber saw, 84–85, 85
Sandbox, back-yard, 47
Sanding, 95

Sawbuck, rugged, 72
Sawhorses & plank, 60
Saws, and sawing, 84–85
Scooter planes, 54–55
Screws, 93–94
Sealing, 95
Serving board 6-pack, 5
Sewing center, 66–67
Shaping & smoothing wood, 86
Shellac, 95
Shelves, toy, in hanging boxes, 50
Skimboard, 66
Slide-on bookend, 18
Small fry's desk, 42–43
Smoothing & shaping wood, 86
Smoothing plane, 86
Softwood plywood, buying, 82
Spice rack, 7
Splines, wooden, 90–91
Spool organizer, 63
Stacking wine rack, 14
Stains, 95
Stepstool carryall, 11
Stepstool chair, 16–17
Storage bed, 38
Swedish ribbstol, 69
Swing, horse, 44–45
Swing, outdoor seat, 57

Table & play-block chairs, 53
Table & stool set, compact, 24–25
Tables, 20–21, 24–29, 31–37, 41, 53, 61
Table saw, 85
Tape measure, steel, 83
T-bevel, sliding, 83
Techniques & tools, 81–95
Tile-top table, 28
Tile trivet, 10
Tools & techniques, 81–95
Tote boxes, 10
Towel rack, bathroom, 12
Toys, 40, 44–47, 54–57, 58, 64–66
Toy shelves in hanging boxes, 50
Trestle table, 35–37
Trivet, tile, 10
Trompe l'oeil coffee table, 33
Twist drills, 87

Varnish, 95

Waterproof glue, 94
Water stains, 95
Whirligig, 73
White (polyvinyl) glue, 94
Wind-up toy boat, 40
Wine racks, 14–15
Wing dividers, 83–84
Wood, buying, 81–82
Wood repairs, 95
Workbench, easy-to-make, 59
Work table, mural, 41

Yard & garden accessories, 70–80